The Interface between Intercession and Holiness

The Interface between Intercession and Holiness

A Reflective Biblical Narrative Perspective

HERMANN YOKONIAH MVULA

RESOURCE *Publications* • Eugene, Oregon

THE INTERFACE BETWEEN INTERCESSION AND HOLINESS
A Reflective Biblical Narrative Perspective

Resource Publications
An Imprint of Wipf and Stock Publishers
199 W. 8th Ave., Suite 3
Eugene, OR 97401

www.wipfandstock.com

PAPERBACK ISBN: 978-1-6667-7869-4
HARDCOVER ISBN: 978-1-6667-7870-0
EBOOK ISBN: 978-1-6667-7871-7

01/31/24

CONTENTS

1   Introduction   1

2   Abraham: A Friend of Yahweh   4

3   Moses: The Servant of Yahweh   15

4   David: A Man after God's Own Heart   36

5   King Solomon: A Darling for Yahweh   66

6   Daniel: God's Faithful Prophet in Captivity   74

7   Ezra: A Puritan Reformer and Yahweh's Patriot   85

8   Jesus: Yahweh's Beloved Son   98

9   Paul: God's Bondservant and Apostle per Excellence   108

10 Conclusion: Jesus, the God Who Interceeds for Us   117

Bibliography   121

1

INTRODUCTION

THIS BOOK IS A biblical theology narrative of how godly people ought to live lives that demonstrate their holy character. Basically, narrative theology is a fairly broad term, but oftentimes it is that approach to theology that primarily looks to the meaning in story. Narrative theology is associated with the idea that we are not primarily to learn principles, rules or laws from Scripture, but rather we are to learn to relate to God, and how to play our part in the greater panorama of our salvation. Narrative theology teaches that the Bible is seen as the story of God's interaction with His people. Supporters of narrative theology maintain that this does not mean the Bible doesn't make propositional truth assertions, but that the primary purpose of Scripture is to record the relationship between God and His people and how we today, in this post-modern world, can continue in this story.[1] The discipline of biblical theology affirms the theological unity of the Old and New Testaments, while recognizing the diversity of the biblical books in terms of content, genre and provenance. Affirming the divinely inspired nature of the whole Bible, the discipline of biblical theology attempts to

---

1. See "What is narrative theology?" | GotQuestions.org (https://bing.com/search/q=biblical+theology+narrative&cvid)(accessed 3 April, 2023).

explain how this remarkable anthology of religious texts conveys a unified theological message.[2]

The book focuses on what it means to be a holy person, what it means to be a peculiar person, what it means to be a priestly person—one who prays and intercedes for others. This is the mission why God called Abraham—so that he and his descendants can offer intercessory prayers for others in the world. This therefore, is demonstrated in this book where we shall discuss a few notable biblical individuals of the nation of Israel whose intercessory character exemplify what it means to be holy. The book consequently takes a keen look at the following biblical personalities: Abraham, Moses, David, Solomon, Daniel, Ezra, Jesus and Paul. These are people who interceded for their brothers and sisters and thereby demonstrating the true character and lifestyle of holiness in wishing good for others, i.e., praying for God's forgiveness, goodness and intervention on behalf of His people.

Critical and reflective reading of Deuteronomy 4:6–8 shows that as a nation Israel would be shaped and characterised by the laws and institutions of the Sinai covenant, and she would be a highly visible exemplary to the nations both as to the nature of the God they worshipped and as to the quality of social justice embodied in their community.[3] This was a deliberate link of Israel's role among the nations to the socio-ethical structure of their corporate life: mission and ethics combined. Israel's mission was to be a model to the nations. Christopher Wright rightly states, "Mission was not a matter of going but being; to be what they were, to live as a people of Yahweh their God in the sight of the nations."[4]

This book begins its survey with a look at the person and character of Abraham, a patriarch and a native of Ur of the Chaldeans in Mesopotamia. He was selected and called by Yahweh

---

2. T. D. Alexander, "Biblical Theology" (https://thegospelcoalition.orgessay.biblical-thelogy/) (accessed 3 April, 2023).

3. McBride, S.D. "Polity of the Covenant People: The Book of Deuteronomy," *Interpretation* 41 (1987), 229–44.

4. Wright, Christopher J.H. *Deuteronomy*. (Grand Rapids, MI: Baker Books, 1996), 13.

to become a father of many nations within which a great nation would arise. Abraham is radically cherished by millions of people as their father—founder of their religion. Judaism traces its roots to him. Christianity traces its roots to him. Islam also claims its roots to him. Both in fleshly terms and spiritual terms, these three so-called monotheistic religious faiths claim their descent from this man. The other biblical personalities follow subsequently, one after the other in each chapter. These are Moses, David, Solomon, Daniel, Ezra, Jesus and Paul. Each chapter is a narrative story of the person and character of each of these individuals demonstrating how they lived their intercessory life thereby exemplifying the life of holiness.

2

ABRAHAM: A FRIEND OF YAHWEH[1]

INTRODUCTION

THE BIBLE DESCRIBES ABRAHAM as a friend of God (2 Chronicle 20: 7; Isaiah 41:8; James 2:23). Abraham came from Ur of the Chaldeans, in Mesopotamia, currently either in Iraq or northern Syria. This man, whose name was initially Abram may literally mean "the father is exalted," or the "exalted father," or "the father of the exalted." He was the first of the great patriarchs of Israel. In the Ancient Near East a patriarch was the leader or ancestor of a family, but Abraham exceeded this status by becoming the progenitor of one specific nation, the Hebrews, as well as of other peoples. Abraham is of profound religious significance because he was the historic ancestor of the twelve tribes, the "seed of Abraham," who regularly described their God as "the God of their forefathers: Abraham, Isaac and Jacob." Theologically, through Abraham, God began to reveal himself, his character and his will for the human

---

1. See 2 Chronicle 20: 7; Isaiah 41:8; James 2:23.

race. Historically, through Abraham, God revealed that He is the God of the past, the present and future, i.e., He is the Eternal God. By virtue of being children of divine promise (Genesis 12:2), the Israelites were living proof of God's existence and power in human society. This general promise was made specific by means of a covenant between God and Abraham (Genesis 15:8–18; 17:1–14), which provided the offspring of the patriarch with a large tract of territory. Abraham was to father many nations (Genesis 17:5), and the covenant that was to be established with him and his seed was to be perpetual in nature. Although coming from a background of polytheism and idolatry at Ur, Abraham had been nurtured in the faith of the one true God by his father Terah.[2] But when he received the LORD's call at a mature stage of his life, he recognized that he had been chosen to implement a specific part of God's plan for human destiny. He was not to fulfill it alone, because the LORD undertook to go with him (Genesis 12:4). He was required to be consistently obedient to God's will, however difficult that might be, and to trust without question the guidance he would receive against the background of the covenant framework. Abraham was not asked to be obedient as a condition of the covenant as true as that was on one hand. Rather, his response in faith was based upon what he might have already known about the God of his ancestors, however little that knowledge might have been at this stage in his life and walk with Yahweh. Hence, it was a matter of free choice. The importance of strict obedience to the LORD's injunctions assumes early prominence in Old Testament theology. Put simply, without unquestioning submission to God's stipulations there could be neither fellowship with the Lord nor blessings poured out upon the covenant people.

2. Scholarly reflection argues that perhaps before God called Abraham, he might have called his father Terah, but due to old age or even little faith, Terah could not proceed with the journey southward from Ur and hence stopped at Haran. And it was soon after Terah's death at Haran (Damascus in Syrian/Padan-Aram) that God then called one of his sons Abraham to proceeding with the divine call and election down to the land of promise.

ABRAHAM, THE FATHER OF MANY NATIONS

The story of Abraham begins in Genesis 11 where it is mentioned that he was one of the three sons of Terah, a patriarch of Ur of the Chaldeans. However, candid portrayal of the story of Abraham begins in Genesis 12 where God calls him to 'leave his family and his kinsmen and go to a land He would show him.' Successively, Genesis chapters 13, 15, 17 and 18 are so full of theological truths in their narratives, bearing God's promises to Abraham, depicting how God continues to reveal himself to Abraham in Canaan as well as during his short-lived sojourn in Egypt. In His initial revelation and promise-making to Abraham, God promises Abraham three very important things in Genesis 12:2–3:

1. Personal Blessing: A great name

2. National Blessing: A great nation

3. Universal Blessing: A great universal redemption

In Genesis 15 and 17, God makes covenant with Abraham and promises him land and descendants. So the promise of God to Abraham of life, land and posterity—through which all the families of the world would be blessed proclaims the beginning of new chapter of God's redemptive acts for a fallen world. Sin had created a chasm and breach between humans and God but God was now revealing a plan to bridge that gap through promising the end from the beginning. Eventually, Abraham's seed will bring salvation and redemption to the entire human race. This threefold promise and Divine plan provide the key to understanding all of biblical faith and human history.

As a father of many nations, Abraham had seven sons beginning with Ishmael (through the maidservant Hagar), Isaac (through Sarah his wife) and the five sons (through Keturah, Abraham's second wife after Sarah passed away). These are the Jews, the Arabs, and the Midianites, among others. All these sons of Abraham became individual nations. Indeed, Abraham was a father of many nations—physical nations that existed and perhaps continue to exist today. However, in spite of this fact that Abraham was a father of many nations, and perhaps a "great nation" (Israel), God's call for him was for the whole world. But his call by God was first a particular call where God's choice of Abraham and his descendants through Isaac, as a son of promise, not through any of the six sons. However, in God's plan of blessing all the families of the world, these other nations through Abraham's other sons are included, just as all the families of the world are included.

ABRAHAM'S INTERCESSORY (PRIESTLY) ROLE

During his sojourn in Canaan, Abraham acted as a priest in chapter 18 of Genesis which this article takes a keen interest as it depicts how godly Abraham was. It can be argued, as we shall do later in this section that godliness in its intrinsic nature has to do with how an individual is able to intercede for others.

Therefore, Yahweh's relationship with Abraham is defined in the course of the history as that of a personal God who grants him land, offspring, abundance, blessing and victory in battle. The Abrahamic cycle presents Abraham as father and religious founder; it defines Israel's claim to the Promised Land and its relationship with and a religious bond between Yahweh and the children of Abraham.

The roots of Israel's history show the importance of justice and righteousness. The earliest traditions present the LORD as the God who does justice and who requires it. Genesis 18:19 makes the remarkable affirmation in the mouth of God in conversation with Abraham that the creation of a community of righteousness and justice was the immediate purpose of Abraham's election. The ultimate purpose was the blessing of the nations, i.e., "what He has promised him." Abraham will surely become a great and powerful nation, and all nations on earth will be blessed through him.[3] "For I have chosen him, so that he will direct his children and his household after him to keep the way of the LORD by doing what

---

3. We have already alluded to this threefold blessing of God to Abraham in the foregoing.

is *right and just* (*sedeq and mispat*), so that the LORD will bring about for Abraham what he has promised him."[4]

The immediate context of the above comprehensive statement of divine purpose is the wickedness of Sodom and Gomorrah and God's planned judgment on those cities. However, what the text focuses on is not just that God has observed their wickedness, but that He has seen and heard the suffering of the oppressed—"the outcry has reached me" (Genesis 18: 20). Christopher Wright argues that "'Outcry' is *sedeq*, almost a technical word for the cry of pain from those who are oppressed or violated."[5] Richard Boyce gives a whole chapter (chapter 3) on the use of this term and its associated verb in the legal setting of the "cry for help" addressed to the authorities by the needy. It would certainly sharpen our understanding of Genesis 18:20 if what God heard from Sodom and Gomorrah was not just "an outcry" but specifically "a cry for help" addressed to Him as the ultimate Judge of all the earth.[6]

Theologically, the essential message drawn from the concept of justice is that the justice of God presents Yahweh as the God who sees and hears the cry of the weak and oppressed, cares about them and takes action on their behalf. Biblically, this is the essential meaning of *sapat*—to act on behalf of the wronged and put things right.[7] That is what we read in Genesis 18:25: "Will not the Judge of the earth do right?" The point above is a rhetorical affirmation as Wright puts it that

> It was unthinkable that the LORD should do otherwise, since His very character is definitive of what is right and just. The LORD himself must act in accordance with what He requires of Abraham and his descendants and household. The same issue is seen during the exodus for Israel. It was the paradigmatic demonstrations of the

---

4. Genesis 18:19.

5. Christopher Wright, *Old Testament Ethics for God's People*, 259.

6. See Richard Boyce, *The Cry to God in the Old Testament*. SBL Dissertation Series, 103. (Atlanta: Scholars Press, 1988).

7. Christopher Wright, *Old Testament Ethics for God's People*, 261ff.

LORD's justice in action, in both senses—judgment and salvation.[8]

Biblical revelation continually affirms that the God of justice must act justly. However, what is so striking about this context in which these verses are found are the intercessory prayers and supplication for Sodom and Gomorrah by Abraham. The drama is as follows:

God had intentions to destroy the two Jordan Valley cities due to their continued wickedness, which had reached unbearable levels. Lot, Abraham's nephew had migrated and settled in these splendor lavished valley cities. So, when God revealed to Abraham his intentions, Abraham remembered that his nephew Lot had settled there and got one of the daughters of the valley cities as a wife and together they had two daughters. Because, by this time Abraham had a lengthy walk with Yahweh, he understood that He is a God of justice and righteousness whose 'eyes do not look on evil'—Habakkuk 1:13, he therefore started interceding for the cities.

It could be argued that it was primarily because his nephew Lot was there. However, his dialogue with God further shows that he was concerned for all the people in the cities. His intercession for them was so thorough that he dialogued with God from step to step trying to understand and invoke God's mercy and grace for the people of the valley. He went on pleading with God on account from at least fifty righteous people all the way down to ten. In each instance, God showed him that He was ready to avert his judgment on Sodom and Gomorrah if there were fifty righteous people, then thirty, then twenty all the way to ten.

Unfortunately, it appears that Sodom and Gomorrah had far much more wicked people than the righteous ones and as such, they had reached a destruction point and stage. In fact, even if God had not come down to destroy these cities, because of their wickedness, they would have acted in self-destruction. When wickedness increases, it reaches a point of self-destruction—where wicked people unleash destruction on each other and hence destroy each

---

8. Christopher Wright, *Old Testament Ethics for God's People*, 261ff.

other. Theologically, it seems out of His sheer Divine grace, only Lot's family found grace in the sight of Yahweh, the God of justice and righteousness.

It is an interesting dialogue between Abraham and God, where we see Abraham interceded for Sodom and Gomorrah. He begins asking for the cities to be spared, if there are but 50 righteous who are in it. He boldly prays, "Far be it from you to do such a thing, to slay the righteous with the wicked, so that the righteous fare as the wicked! Far be it from You! Shall not the Judge of all the earth do right? God agrees that he will not destroy the cities if he finds 50 righteous. Abraham then asks for the city to be spared if there are but 45, he humbly states, "Behold I have taken upon myself to speak to the Lord, who am I but dust and ashes." God agrees to spare for 45 righteous. Abraham asks to spare for 40, God agrees. Abraham again shows humility and more boldness, "Oh let not the Lord be angry, and I will speak, suppose 30 be found," God agrees to spare for 30. Notice here that Abraham began his negotiations by increments of 5, but now asks in increments of 10. Abraham asks to spare for 20, God agrees. Abraham asks to spare for 10, God agrees, and then the LORD went his way.

These were Abraham's negotiatory skills, demonstrating his intercessory stamina. God was willing to listen to his prayers, petition and supplications and avert his plan to destroy Sodom and Gomorrah in response to his intercession. The attitude and posture that God requires of each one of us when we have truly known him is precisely this. This is the attitude and posture that God requires of each one of us when we have truly known Him is precisely this. Indeed, Abraham exemplifies the great privilege of God's covenant people throughout the ages: God has revealed his purposes to them and allows their intercessory voice to be heard in the court of heaven itself.

EXCURSUS: ABRAHAM'S OFFERING OF ISAAC—
THE SIGNIFICANCE OF MOUNT MORIAH

The story of Abraham in the book of Genesis is not complete without his faith being tested by God. Genesis chapter 22:1-19 offers dramatic epic of what it means to be godly, faithful and to trust in Yahweh in all things. After waiting for a long time to have a child—25 years after the promise was made by God, Abraham's wife Sarah, gave birth to a son whom they named Y'isaak, English—Isaac. When Isaac was a teenager or perhaps when he was in his early 20s, God demanded Abraham to have his son offered as a sacrifice to him. No doubt, this brought anguish on Abraham who had waited for such a long time to have a child of his own with his wife Sarah.

The narrative shows that when God commanded Abraham to offer his only son Isaac as sacrifice to God on a place he would show him in the region of Moriah, Abraham took with him son Isaac and his servants plus firewood. However, on their way when they had left the servants at some point, Isaac asked his father about the sacrificial lamb? He said, "Father behold the fire and the wood, but where is the lamb for the sacrifice?" No doubt, as a father, who had this son as the only child, Abraham might have been troubled in heart. But he found courage and responded to his son's question: "God himself will provide the lamb," or "God will provide the lamb for himself," or "God will provide the lamb himself." Abraham's response was the ultimate manner in which faith ought to be in God's children. He might have had no idea of what will happen but he faithfully and trustfully responded that Yahweh-Jireh will provide. And indeed, seeing his readiness to offer his only son, God stopped Abraham from sacrificing his son and offer, instead not a lamb, but a ram which was trapped in a thicket.

Some theological analysis shows that the place that Abraham made a shrine to sacrifice his son Isaac, is the exact place—Golgotha—that God's Son offered himself as sacrifice for the sins of humanity. This is the significance of Mount Moriah that the place where God showed Abraham to sacrifice his son, a son that he had waited for 25 years after God promised him, was the exact place that God Himself had prepared to offer the Ultimate Sacrifice—Lamb of God that would take away the sin of the world.[9] Only Yahweh, the God of history—past, present and future could keep the exact locations, places, positions that signify something bigger. So, the offering of Abraham's son Isaac, was a type of the offering that God had prepared beforehand, that His only begotten Son, born of a woman in the fullness of time,[10] would be offered, breathed his last and pronounce, 'it is finished' on Mount Moriah, thousands of years later. One intriguing motif in this story is that what God commands us or asks from us, is what He Himself can or would do. Indeed, Mount Moriah is the Jerusalem site itself. And that very point on the Mountain is the very point that God would sacrifice His Only Begotten Son, Jesus Christ. The Moriah region, and specifically Mount Moriah—Jerusalem also known as Zion, is indeed the center of the world. No wonder the so-called three Monotheistic religions or faiths—all of them claiming descent from Abraham, scramble to have control over it.

CONCLUSION

In Genesis 18, God shows his favor towards Abraham by appearing to him in the form of three travelers. During their meeting, Abraham intercedes for Sodom, asking God if He would destroy the city if even 10 righteous people live there. This is one of the favorite accounts in the Bible and especially in Genesis, as God's dealings with Sodom are both strict and merciful at the same time. Abraham intercedes for Sodom and Gomorrah.

Therefore, Genesis 18:16–33 shows that Abraham pleads with God for the cities of Sodom and Gomorrah. In this passage, first, we see that true prayer begins with God, verse 17, where God reveals to Abraham that he is going to go down and see if the sin in Sodom is grievous. God engages with Abraham "a friend of God"

9. See John 2:29.

10. Galatians 4:4. Cf, Seed of the Woman in Genesis 3:15.

and tells him that he is going to destroy the cities. God does not say specifically what he will do, but says He will go and see, and "I will know." Abraham who knows all the sins of the city, knows the cities are doomed and thus begins to plead with God, because he recognizes God's mercy. Verses 22–32 detail the conversation of God and Abraham showing the back and forth negotiations between Abraham and God. It is quite a very interesting conversation. There are thus a few lessons from this passage that God is revealing to us and requires of us if we are to be truly. These are:

1. True prayer starts with God—it is about His will and intentions not ours;

2. We should be humble and know their place or standing before God—we speak to God the Creator and Ruler of the whole universe;

3. We should be very bold when appealing to God's gracious forgiveness for ourselves as well as for others;

4. In the story of Abraham and offering his son Isaac, God was exemplifying his own story for the love of the world;

5. We should be very persistent in all kinds of prayers until we receive an answer.

There enigma of the story of Sodom and Gomorrah will never cease. whether the violent mob surrounding Lot's house were demanding to engage in sexual violence against Lot's guests or whether it was homosexuality or another transgression, such as the act of inhospitality towards visitors, their action and the cry of the people had reached proportional levels for God's intervention and He did it, by destroying these wicked cities in the Jordan River Valley. What God did to these cities is an example of what he would do to any community of people whose wickedness reaches proportional levels of His Heavenly abode.

Therefore, Abraham's holy stamina is demonstrated or manifested through his incessant intercession for the family of his nephew together with the nations of the Jordan Valley. It was this very attitude and posture of Abraham that God was pleased and continued to commit Himself to fulfilling His promises made earlier to Abraham. Abraham demonstrates what it means to know God and what it means to walk with Him, i.e., becoming like him in holy character. What is means to be holy could largely be manifested through interceding for those who are continuing to live in their sins and wickedness. Hence, Abraham sets the pace for what true godliness and holiness entail: living lives of full devotion to God and His redemptive mission on earth—interceding for all humanity so that they come to the true knowledge of Yahweh, the God revealed to Abraham and his posterity as recorded in biblical scriptures.

3

MOSES: THE SERVANT OF YAHWEH[1]

INTRODUCTION

MOSES WAS ONE OF the greatest figures in the life of the nation of Israel. Born some generations after Abraham, Isaac and Jacob, Moses towers high as national leader, a prophet and a priest[2] in the history of Israel. Some scholars attribute Judaism to have been founded by Moses.[3] The voluminous first five books of the Bible, the *Torah*, or Pentateuch are traditionally ascribed to his authorship.[4] One of the psalms, Psalm 90 is also ascribed to Moses as the author.[5] According to rabbinic tradition, as attested by Rabbi Mendy

1. See Joshua 1: 1–2.

2. This chapter proves that Moses played a priestly role during his time as the leader of the Israelites.

3. See *Judaism: Founder, Beliefs* (https://www.history.com) (accessed on 5 March, 2021). See also *BBC-Religions-Judaism* (https://www.bbc.co.uk) (accessed on 5 March, 2021).

4. See *BBC-Religions-Judaism* (https://www.bbc.co.uk) (accessed on 5 March, 2021).

5. See "Did Moses Write Psalm 90? Biblical Hermeneutics Stack Exchange" (s.stackexchange.com) (accessed online on 5 March, 2021). See also

Wineberg, he was immensely handsome[6] and powerful,[7] and his countenance was like that of an angel.[8]

Moses is the most important Jewish prophet or figure. He is traditionally credited with writing the Torah and with leading the Israelites out of Egypt and across the Red Sea. In the book of Exodus, he is born during a time when the Pharaoh of Egypt had ordered every male Hebrew to be killed. Over a thousand years after Abraham, the Jews were living as slaves in Egypt. Moses led the Jews out of slavery in Egypt and led them to the Holy Land that God had promised their forefathers. God sent Moses back to Egypt to demand the release of the Israelites from slavery. The escape of the Hebrew people from Egypt is remembered by Jews every year in the festival of Passover. To protect Moses, his mother puts him in a basket and threw him down afloat the Nile River, where he is ultimately found by Pharaoh's daughter who adopted him as her own and raised him in Pharaoh's palaces where he got higher education in history, literature, art, music, etc.[9] Acts 7:22 says, "Moses was educated in all the wisdom of the Egyptians and was powerful in speech and action."

Scriptures tell us that Moses was adopted and raised in the palaces of Egypt—looking forward to becoming a Pharaoh someday because at that time Pharaoh did not have any male child but daughters only. During that period, Egyptian tradition allowed only the male sons of the Pharaoh to ascend onto the throne and become the king. Therefore, since Pharaoh did not have a male child, Moses was being trained and groomed to ascend the throne when the Pharaoh dies—descends to join the ancestors and become part of the divinities, i.e., becomes a god. So, tradition and other

---

David Guzik, "Psalm 90—The Prayer of Moses in the Wilderness" (*Enduring Word Bible Commentary*, Psalm 90, 2016) (accessed on 5 March, 2021).

6. See Shemot Rabba 1: 26.

7. See Nedarim 38a.

8. See Pirkei D'rabi Eliezer 48.

9. See John, Ritenbaugh, "What the Bible says about Education of Moses" (bibletools.org) (accessed on 22 March 2023).

extra-biblical literature show that Moses was very educated in all wisdom, literature, politics and art of ancient Egypt—Egyptology.

THE PERSON OF MOSES: HIS NATIONAL DUTIES TO THE PEOPLE OF ISRAEL

One of Judaism's great figures was the man called Moses, *Moshe Rabbenu* in Hebrew, i.e., "Moses our teacher." Moses taught a lot of things, i.e., instructions to the Hebrew people. The first five books of the Bible are traditionally ascribed to him. Moses was the channel between God and the Hebrews, through whom the Hebrews received a basic charter for living as God's people. That basic charter, grounded in the Decalogue, was to help Israelites live their lives worthy of being the life to the nations.

Moses was the son of the tribe of Levi named Amram and his mother was Jochebed, a daughter of a Levite too. Moses was the last-born child of his parents with Miriam and Aaron as his elder sister and elder brother. Born at a time when Pharaoh and his officials in Egypt had issued a decree to have all the male born babies of Hebrews to be killed. However, since God's plans cannot be thwarted by anyone, Moses was miraculously spared by Yahweh's gracious intervention to the extent that instead of being killed, after he was recognized as a Hebrew child, he was spared and adopted by Pharaoh's daughter as her own son. What happened was that when Moses, her youngest child was born, Jochebed hid him for three months until she could hide him no longer. To save her Moses' life, she waterproofed a basket and put the child in it and placed him in a basket and put him in the flow of River Nile. Since Moses was then adopted by Pharaoh's daughter, he was raised in the very palace of Pharaoh where the murdering horde order on all Hebrew children had originated.

Consequently, Moses grew up in the palaces of Pharaoh. However, despite growing up in such luxurious opulent atmosphere, Moses seemed to have compassion for his fellow Hebrew people who at that time were suffering servitude in the hands of the Egyptians as their slave masters tortured them for many years.

This happened when a new dynasty of Pharaohs who did not know Joseph arose.[10] Therefore, Moses initially lived in Egypt as a prince for 40 years before his flight to Midian after killing an Egyptian. However, despite speaking of his flight from Egypt to Midian' it was God's grace to offer deliverance for his enslaved people, the descendants of Abraham, his friend.

Indeed, Exodus narratives indicate that the turning point in the life of Moses seems to be when he found a Hebrew man being beaten up by an Egyptian and Moses took the side of a fellow Hebrew and killed the Egyptian. A few days later or just a day later, he found the same Hebrew man quarreling with a fellow Hebrew and Moses tried to reconcile them. Unfortunately, hell broke loose when this particular Hebrew, whom Moses had rescued from an Egyptian the previous day, rhetorically screamed: "Who made you ruler and judge over us? You want to kill me as you killed an Egyptian yesterday."? With these words, Moses knew that it was or it would no longer be a secret that he killed the Egyptian.[11] So, Pharaoh wanted to kill Moses. But he fled to Midian where upon arrival, he found grace in the household of a priest named Jethro in this desert territory. Later on, after staying with Jethro who had seven daughters, Moses was married one of his daughters named Zipporah.

Owing his upbringing in the palaces of Pharaoh in Egypt, Moses was a gifted, well-trained person. However, his true greatness was probably not based on his giftedness and education; but on his personal experience of and relationship with Yahweh. As time went by, Moses, the former stammering man who killed an Egyptian understood his preservation and destiny as coming from the grace of a merciful LORD who had given him another chance. Moses had an understanding spirit and a forgiving heart because he knew how much Yahweh had forgiven him. He was truly humble because he recognized that his gifts and strength came from Yahweh. It is not an overstatement therefore to argue that, because of the uniqueness of his situation, Yahweh had prepared

10. See Exodus 1:8–14.
11. See Exodus 2:11–13.

Moses beforehand to function in a number of roles. As Yahweh's agent in the deliverance of the Hebrews, he was their prophet and leader. As mediator of the covenant, he was the founder of the community. As interpreter of the covenant, he was an organizer and legislator. As intercessor for the people, he was their priest. Moses had a special combination of gifts and graces that made it impossible to replace him. Although his successor, Joshua, and the Priest Eleazar, the son of Aaron, tried to do so, together they did not measure up to him. Later prophets were great men who spoke out of the spirit that Moses had, but they were not called to function in so many roles. As tradition claims, he was indeed the greatest of the prophets, and, as history shows, few of humanity's great personalities outrank him in influence. And many in our own contemporary histories would do better because they have a precursor of an example of what it means to be a leader—learning from Moses' lifestyles—to which Moses himself did not have any example to look to.

The Exodus Duty of Moses: Deliverance of the People of Israel

While tending the flock of his father-in-law Jethro in the vicinity of Mount Sinai, one day Yahweh, the God of Israel's forefathers—Abraham, Isaac, and Jacob appeared to him in a burning bush. He spoke to him assuring him that He knows him, he knows the suffering and tribulation of His people in Egypt, and that He had come down to rescue them.[12] The Exodus narratives demonstrate how God through the human agent of Moses delivered his people from State oppression, repression, exploitation and dehumanization in Egypt. Very pertinent to the study of Exodus beginning with chapter 3 demonstrates God's concern and demonstration of his grace and love toward those who are powerless. Some of great theological ideals found in Exodus 3 are the following theological

---

12. See Exodus 3: 1–10.

motifs and ethical trajectories about Yahweh whose activities can be observed as:

1. Yahweh sees the people's sufferings;
2. Yahweh hears the people's cry;
3. Yahweh knows the people's sorrows;
4. Yahweh moves to offer help;
5. Yahweh delivers the marginalized and oppressed and exploited;
6. Yahweh offers better living conditions

The passage shows that not only was God intimately aware of the troubles of his people in Egypt, but he would eventually act on their behalf. The Divine responses above demonstrate his concern and power to aid those in oppression. It must be pointed out that in His deliverance activities, Yahweh engages human agents to accomplish His plans of deliverance from oppression.

So when God was talking to Moses about His plans to deliver Israelites from Egypt, Moses thought he would be a spectator as God transported His people out of Egypt. But it was not so. He was to be the very agent God wants to use in that mission. God's methodology in whatever his mission is reaching people through people. After a lengthy discussion between Moses and Yahweh the God of his forefathers, Abraham, Isaac and Jacob, Moses accepted to go back to Egypt to play the role of deliverer of the Hebrews. Narratives in Exodus chapters 4 through 18 depict a conflict between Yahweh, the almighty God of the Hebrews, who is the Creator of the whole universe, and Pharaoh and his gods. In all that, Moses' God won the battle and the Hebrew people were released from bondage of slavery by Yahweh through the media of Moses as the exodus leader.

Therefore, what unfolded in the events that begun in Exodus chapter 3 manifests the power of Yahweh in saving his people who were under oppression in Egypt. Exodus narratives continue God's self-revelation, not only as a remote national God, but as a God with universal powers and cosmic world-wide mission, and that he had partially started demonstrating his faithfulness in keeping the promises He had made to Israel's forefathers—Abraham, Isaac and Jacob. Yahweh is the Promise-making God, Promise-keeping God, and Promise-Fulfilling God. So by defeating Egyptians, who were the world's super power then, God demonstrated beyond doubt that His powers know no human authority in the universe.

Through the initial encounter with God in the burning bush, that Moses witnessed burning but unconsumed, his curiosity aroused, he approached the scene, only to hear a voice ordering him to come no closer and to remove his sandals because he was standing on holy ground. The voice identified himself as that of the God of his ancestors, the three patriarchs of Israel: Abraham, Isaac and Jacob. Moses was told that God was about to deliver his people from Egypt and to bring them into the Promised Land. Moses himself is to be chosen the instrument for this purpose. A long dialogue between God and Moses ensued in which Moses protested his unworthiness and God repeatedly reassured him that He would be with him through that divine mission. Reluctantly, Moses accepted to go back to Egypt to begin the deliverance process by engaging the Pharaoh and his cabinet. Later on, Moses realized that his very life was God's call to divine mission.

Through Exodus narratives, we can observe how God liberated the children of Israel from bondage of slavery in Egypt. This was intrinsically God's political move which involved the interests of the Egyptian kingdom under the Pharaoh, and the nation of Israel itself under Moses, the adopted grandson of Pharaoh. Yahweh, the God revealed in the Bible, is the Liberator, Deliverer, and as we study theology, which is his "liberation and deliverance story," we deal with the very core of Biblical faith—liberation from bondage, both spiritual and physical. The Exodus narratives demonstrate that God's deliverance from all kinds of oppression takes place when He finds willing partners to work with. And Moses was God's tool and means to liberate and deliver Abraham's descendants—whom God had committed himself to the latter in his self-maledictory oath he enacted in Genesis 15.

Constitutional Duty of Moses: The Decalogue and the Law for Israel's Personal and National Life

Moses organized the Hebrew people to be nation whose role, according to biblical witness, was to be "a light to the nations" so that all the nations may be saved.[13] Although time undoubtedly enhanced the portrait of Moses, a basic picture emerges from the biblical sources themselves. Five times the narratives claim that Moses kept written records (Ex. 17:14; 24:4; 34:27–28; Num. 33:2; and Deut. 31:9, 24–26). Even with a generous interpretation of the extent of these writings, they do not amount to more than a fifth of the total Pentateuch. Moses received the Decalogue from God, mediated the Covenant, and began the process of rendering and codifying supplemental interpretations of the Covenant stipulations which would government Israel, at both individual and national levels. Undoubtedly, he kept some records, and they served as the core of the growing corpus of law and tradition. In a general sense, therefore, the first five books of the Hebrew Bible are traditionally described as Mosaic. Without him as graced by God, there would have been no constituted nation of Israel and perhaps no collection known as Torah.

A few days after their being delivered, Moses took them through the region of Sinai and almost on the exact place that God had appeared to Moses some weeks, months or years earlier, He appeared to the whole nation of Israel, giving Moses the Decalogue, as a moral code, through which the people of Israel would live by. The Decalogue was given by God to Israel as a way of molding them into a nation that He had promised Abraham, Isaac and Jacob respectively, in what is commonly known as the Abrahamic covenant. Therefore, Moses was such a figure who played this great role of God's calling of a national people, the Israelites whose mandate was to fulfill what He had initially promised Abraham. So Israel became God's special people, a peculiar people, a holy nation, a royal priesthood, so that she might be the light to the nations.[14]

13. See Isaiah 42:6; 49:6; 60:3.

14. See for instance, Exodus 19: 5–6; Deuteronomy 7:6; 14:2; Isaiah 42:6;

The instructions in the books of Exodus, Leviticus, Numbers and Deuteronomy became the capstone through which this new nation was to live by upholding God's ethical, moral, ceremonial and civil laws or instructions. To date, wherever Jews are, they treasure these first five books of the Bible commonly called *torah* in Hebrew, which literally means "instructions."[15] The giving of the Decalogue to Israel is about instructions on relationships. The vertical relationship entails man's obligation to God and the horizontal relationships that entail man's relationship to his neighbor. With the extrapolation and exposition of the Decalogue in the subsequent sections in the book of Exodus and the books of Leviticus, Numbers and Deuteronomy, the more ground of the laws to govern the nation of Israel and by extension all other nations, are put in place.

On confirmation of the covenant, Moses and the people faced the task of living by the stipulations. This called for interpretations of the commands, and so Moses began issuing ordinances for specific situations. Many of these he drew from the case law of his day, but insight as to their selection and application probably came in the "tent of meeting" (a simple sanctuary tent pitched outside the camp), where Yahweh spoke to Moses "face to face, as a man speaks to his friend." The breaches of the covenant necessitated means of atonement, which in turn meant provision of a priesthood to function at sacrifices and in worship. The essentials of the whole Hebrew cult, according to tradition, originated at Sinai, the very place where Moses had initially encountered God in a burning bush. To consolidate good governance among Israelites, at his father-in-law, Jethro's suggestion Moses instituted a system of judges and hearings to regulate the civil aspects of the community. This could be said to be the institution of the legal system in ancient Israel. Thus, Moses had a political duty to constitutionally organize the 12 tribes into a holy nation of Yahweh, governed by Yahwistic precepts.

49:6, among others.

15. See Joseph Blenkinsopp, *Wisdom and Law in the Old Testament: The Ordering of Life in Israel and Early Judaism* (Oxford: Oxford University Press, 1995).

The Intercessory Duty of Moses: Praying and Pleading with God not to Destroy the Disobedient Israel

One of Moses' most remarkable characteristics was his concern for the Hebrews, in spite of their stubborn and rebellious ways. When they reverted to worshipping a golden calf, Yahweh was ready to disown them and begin anew with Moses and his descendants. Moses rejected the offer and later, when pleading for the forgiveness of the people, he even asked to have his own name blotted out of Yahweh's book of remembrance if the LORD would not forgive them.

The sequential chronology of what happened is as in the following manner. After Moses had shared with the people the Book of the Covenant and led them in the covenant of confirmation, he entered the cloud as he went up on the Mountain to receive the instructions for the tabernacle. After he disappeared, the people soon fell into blatant idolatry. This is the story of the Golden Calf whose cutting edge is the penetrating insight that religion itself can sometimes become a means to disobedience. This is what happened to the people of Israel when Moses, their leader and authoritative figure, with his mesmeric charisma, was absent from them for 40 days when he was on the mountain with God. The story of Israel and the Golden calf has eternal truths for all ages. It may be argued that coupled with their frail human nature, the quality of Israelites' faith was such that the only way the law could even begin to work was for it to be personified, or caught up, in a charismatic authoritative figure to whom blind, unthinking, and absolute loyalty could be given. Therefore, when the people saw that Moses was too long in coming down from the mountain, they confronted Aaron with the cry, "Come, make us gods who will go before us. As for this fellow Moses who brought us out of Egypt, we don't know what has happened to him."[16]

Then Aaron, whom God had appointed to speak for Moses due to the latter's own reluctance to obey God's call, made them a god in place of God. Frank Carver argues that

16. Exodus 32:1.

What is fascinating in this story is that Israelites had deified "the now absent" Moses so he had to be replaced immediately. The result was a religious orgy, a worship that was highly sensual, for after they "sacrificed burnt offerings and presented fellowship offering. . .they sat down to eat and drink and got up to indulge in revelry."[17]

Critical analysis of the passage shows that after Aaron had made the golden calf, blasphemously, the children of Israel effectively broke the first commandment, the second, and the third.[18] Israel's breaking of the second command was a slap in God's face. How could they quickly forget that it was God who brought them out of slavery in Egypt, and then proclaim, affirm and singly shout, "These are the gods that brought you out of bondage of slavery in Egypt, oh Israel?" Children of Israel, i.e., this was a direct affront to Yahweh their God, who has just delivered them from bondage in Egypt, a few days earlier.

Consequently, it can be argued that such a story has a cutting-edge truth that most of the world's so-called religions could truly be a means to disobedience. A number of world's religions and cultic elements owe their allegiance to their founders whose teachings are the domain for the people to follow. Too often people place such figures on a deified pedestal and delegate their responsibilities before God, and therefore their spiritual freedom, to their benevolent tyranny. They "listen" to them and they are to guarantee their relation to God. Hence, they obey a god-substitute.[19] This is the reason why some people strongly argue that Christianity is not a religion; rather it is a relationship; man's personal relationship

17. Exodus 32:6. See also Frank G. Carver, "The Quest for the Holy: The Darkness of God" in *Wesleyan Theological Journal, Volume 23, Number 1 and 2* (Spring-Fall, 1988), 16.

18. The first command— "you shall have no other god beside me." The second command, "You shall not make anything under the sun. . ." the third, "You shall not bow down to any. . ."

19. Frank G. Carver, "The Quest for the Holy: The Darkness of God" in *Wesleyan Theological Journal*, Volume 23, Number 1 and 2 (Spring-Fall, 1988), 15.

with God through the Son Jesus Christ, characterized by worshipping him in spirit and in truth.[20]

Based on the foregoing discussion, the problem with humanity is the tendency to always want to worship something they can see or touch. This is what God forbids. He is above all and anything man can imagine. That means God is beyond any representation by anything that man can make. That is the whole essence of the first and second commandments:[21] "You have no other gods before me." Why, because any other god(s) will result in a different way of worship and he or they will require different ethical and moral conducts. It is also pertinent as the second commandment forbids: "You shall not make for yourself an idol. . ." Christopher Wright argues by commenting that,

> The prohibition of idols in Israel was not because they were material whereas God is spiritual, or because they were visible whereas God is invisible. It was primarily because they were lifeless, impotent and (especially) dumb, whereas God of Israel was living, active and one who speaks. That is why the only image that was 'allowed' was the one God had designed and created himself—the image of God, man himself. It is this kind of thinking, living, choosing, and speaking, moral agent, who alone reflects the living God of the Old Testament.[22]

This means that any attempt to represent God in static or lifeless object, the Golden Calf inclusive, even a human statue, reduces God and denies the most fundamental thing about him. This is not only a theological or religious issue. It is a deep ethical command, for a false view of God would destroy the central foundation of ethics as well, and people will not worship him in the splendor of His holiness. The implication for this is that only the living God of history, Yahweh, He alone has acted in the history of the nation

20. John 4:28.

21. See http://www.thewordisalive.co.uk/OT/Exodus/Exodus32.pdf (accessed on 26th February 2018).

22. Christopher J.H Wright, *Living as the People of God: The Relevance of Old Testament Ethics* (Leicester: Inter-Varsity Press, 1983), 31.

of Israel, could initiate, shape and motivate true worship of any people. Consequently, anything other than that easily becomes blasphemy and idolatry.

A similar story of the Golden calves is found in 1 Kings 11:26–40 and 1 Kings 12:26–33 and 13:33. Of great import here is what Christopher Wrights argues about Jeroboam's sin being subordinating religious observance and traditions to political ends. Critical reading of scripture shows that the Northern kingdom began and ended with a word of prophecy from Abijah, who first, predicting Jeroboam's successful revolt against Rehoboam. Second, promising an enduring dynasty on condition of his obedience. Finally, pronouncing his doom in punishment for his policy of religious pragmatism. Religious pragmatism is the very essence of the debacle of religion as a means to disobedience. Jeroboam erected Golden Calves at the northern and southern ends of his kingdom, i.e., Dan and Bethel, appointed shrines and priests, those who were not from the Levite tribe, surrogate festivals, i.e., a mixture of original and innovative actions. Analysis of this story shows that it all began thus:

> And Jeroboam thought to himself, "The kingdom will now likely revert to the house of David. If these people go up to offer sacrifice at the temple of the LORD in Jerusalem, they will again give their allegiance to their lord, Rehoboam king of Judah. They will kill me and return to King Rehoboam." After seeking advice, the king made two golden calves. He said to the people, "It is too much for you to go up to Jerusalem. Here are your gods, O Israel, who brought you up out of Egypt."[23]

Jeroboam thought to himself. It all begun by his rationalization of the un-established or unfounded problem. One would ask, "Who told him that God was not able to have the people of the north loyal to his kingdom?" Who told him that the people would kill him? Jeroboam did not have confidence in the divine promise given to him through prophet Abijah, and thus took actions that

---

23. Christopher J.H Wright, *Living as the People of God: The Relevance of Old Testament Ethics* (Leicester: Inter-Varsity Press, 1983), 31.

forfeited the divine basis for his kingship. Consequently, through his baseless problem based on his rationalization, Jeroboam was led to the same old Aaronic sin of the Golden Calf.

Therefore, in his rationalization of the unfounded and baseless things, Jeroboam harnessed the existing religious traditions to his political ambition, and to create new ones wherever the interests of his new independent kingdom required it. In doing all this, Jeroboam turned the faith of Israel into a tool of royal policy, and thereby rendered it idolatrous. It is seen here that Jeroboam's royal and political policy promoted violation of the second commandment and inevitably led Israel's violation of the first commandment as well. Then it opened the door for entrance of full pagan practices into Israel's religious rites. Critical reflection of this story shows that Jeroboam foolishly abandoned religious principles for political expediency and in so doing forfeited the promise given him by God through the prophet. It should be noted that Jeroboam stood on the same promises God had made to David. However, whereas David trusted God's ways and upholding his kingdom, Jeroboam did not and he lost it.

THE TOWERING FIGURE OF MOSES: HIS UNRELENTING INTERCESSION FOR ISRAEL DEMONSTRATING HIS HOLY CHARACTER AND HUMILITY

Israel had forgotten that for the maintaining of her relationship the torah had been given. They were to live their lives by the covenant-will of God, to live under its judgment, and thus be drawn to rely on the God of the Exodus and the Sinai, i.e., the God of all grace. God's grace is the ultimate foundation of our ethical existence, lifestyles and true worship which is in spirit and in truth. The problem is as Walter Martin faithfully reminds us:

> It has been wisely observed that 'a man who will not stand for something is quite likely to fall for almost anything.'. . . Elected to have the ramparts of biblical

Christianity as taught by the apostles, defended by the
church fathers, rediscovered by the reformers.. . .[24]

The theme of God's offer of grace implies a theological theme of
Israel's sin and his willingness to forgive.[25] God was angry by the
people's idolatry and worship of the Golden Calf so soon after their
deliverance from Egypt and following their avowed agreement to
the covenant and its stipulations based on the Decalogue. Consequently, God commanded Moses to go down to *"your* people,
whom *you* brought out of the land of Egypt." Ironically, God had
repeatedly referred to Israel as "*my* people")[26] whom "*I* brought out
of the land of Egypt."[27] But after their fall into idolatry by worshiping the golden calf, God rejects them and declared that Israelites are
Moses' people. Now, these are *Moses'* people whom *Moses* brought
out of Egypt. The split of God and Israel from one another seems
mutual.[28]

After His denial of the ownership of the people, God's statement to Moses was startling and terrifying: "Now let me alone, so
that . . . I may consume them.[29]" Here, God resolved to destroy
all the Israelites and raised another people through Moses: "I will
make you a great nation" (Exodus 32:10). Apparently, God offers to
Moses the chance to become the new Abraham, the sole originator

24. Walter Martin, *Kingdom of the Cults*, edited by Ravi Zacharias, (Minneapolis, Bethany House Publishers, 2003), 18.

25. For more information on God's saving and forgiving grace, see Randy
Maddox, *Responsible Grace: John Wesley's Practical theology* (Nashville, TN:
Kingswood Books, 1994). See also Lodahl, Michael Lodahl, *The Story of God:
Wesleyan Theological and Biblical Narrative* (Kansas City, MO: Beacon Hill
Press, 1994).

26. Exodus 3:7, 10; 5:1; 6:7; 7:4, 16; 8:1, 8, 20–23, 9:1, 13, 17; 10:3; 12:31;
19:5–6; 22:25.

27. Exodus 3:17; 6:6–7; 18:1, 12; 20:2; 29:46.

28. This is what Michael Lodahl insinuates as consequences of sin or the
Fall, i.e., shift of responsibilities. This could yet be one of the radical theological
motifs derived from this story. See Michael Lodahl, *The Story of God: Wesleyan
Theological and Biblical Narrative*, (Kansas City, MO: Beacon Hill Press, 1994),
76–79.

29. Exodus 32:10.

of a whole new people who will be a substitute for the destroyed Israelites.[30] However, despite the divine offer Moses denies himself the opportunity to become a new Abraham. In fact Moses humbly asked God to blot him out of the face of the earth if he does not relent from his anger. Instead, he intercedes for Israel with three strong reasons why the LORD should not carry out the planned destruction of Israelites:[31]

1. Remember, these are not my people. They are "your people," LORD, whom "you brought out . . . of Egypt" (32:11).

2. Destroying your own people, Israel, in the wilderness would be bad for your international reputation. What would the Egyptians say? (32:12).

3. Remember the promises of land and descendants that you made to Abraham, Isaac and Israel/Jacob long ago. God, you always keep your promises! (32:13).

Moses used three critical issues to dissuade God from carrying out his intended plan of blotting out Israel from the face of the earth:

1. God's intrinsic faithfulness,

2. God's international reputation,

3. God's irrevocable relationship with Israel's forefathers.

Like the apostle Paul who wished that he himself was accursed for the sake of his people, Israelites,[32] thousands of year later, Moses asked God to remove his name from the Torah[33] if He would not forgive Israelites and keep going with them. Rabbi Mendy Wineberg, asks,

30. Dennis Olson, "Exodus 32:1–14 Commentary" (Accessed from http://www.biblia.work/sermons/exodus-321-14-commentary-by-dennis-olson/ (accessed on 26th February, 2018).

31. Dennis Olson, "Exodus 32:1–14 Commentary" (Accessed from http://www.biblia.work/sermons/exodus-321-14-commentary-by-dennis-olson/ (accessed on 26th February, 2018).

32. See Romans 9:3.

33. See Exodus 32:32.

"How could Moses give up his portion in the Torah, which he was so deeply connected to, for the sake of a people who had just performed idolatry, the most serious of sins? Because Moses' connection to his people— including the greatest sinners—ran even deeper than his connection to Torah."[34]

Therein, lies Moses's holy love character which thrusted him to appeal to God's holy love and mercy for the patriarchs. Herein lies what Jesus urges us—"to love our enemies, to bless them and to pray for them."[35] In his assessment, Kenneth Harris notes that Moses responds to the LORD's statement about destroying the people and making a nation out of him by appealing to God's reputation among the gentiles whom God intends to bless through Israel (Genesis 12:2–3, Exodus 19:60) and his promises to Abraham.[36] Here, Moses' intercession focuses on the LORD's words when he refers to Israel as "your people, whom you have brought out of the land of Egypt."[37]

It is very interesting to observe that in the past Moses was not successful in changing God's mind as observed during his call.[38] However, when advocating for others and therefore denying his own interests of becoming the nation through his descendants, and appealing to the grace and mercy of God, Moses managed to appeal to God. It is very remarkable that in response to Moses' intercession for Israelites, "the LORD changed his mind about the disaster that he planned to bring on his people."[39] God's response to Moses' intercession is to reaffirm the covenant (34:1–28). In

34. See Rabbi Mendy Wineberg, "What the Bible says about Moses as a Statesman" (bibletools.org) Likkutei Sichot, vol. 21, p. 176; (accessed on 22 March 2023).

35. Matthew 5: 43–48.

36. Kenneth Harris, "Exodus," 197. Accessed from http://www.thewordisalive.co.uk/OT/Exodus/Exodus32.pdf (Accessed online on 26th February, 2018).

37. http://www.thewordisalive.co.uk/OT/Exodus/Exodus32.pdf (Accessed on 26th February, 2018).

38. See the call of Moses in Exodus 3:7–4:17.

39. Exodus 32:14.

many ways this is a brief re-enactment of Exodus chapters 19–24. God manifests himself (vv. 5–7), offers his presence and protection (v. 10), stipulates what the people's side of the agreement will entail (vv. 11–26), and directs that the covenant be put in writing (vv. 27–28). Interestingly, this promulgation of the covenant is one-sided. God merely states that he is willing to go on with the previous relationship even though it has been technically dissolved by disobedience of the descendants of Abraham, his friend. Here again, God's maledictory oath made during his covenant with Abraham in Genesis 15 comes into play.

The Exodus narrative in these chapters shows the theme of God's grace, i.e., God reaching out to redeem and forgive his people. In fact, intrinsic to God's grace and forgiveness motifs, is the theme of intercession. Moses did interceded for the people just as Abraham had done for Sodom and Gomorrah in the past. God's people must exercise the priestly role, i.e., interceding for others. Intercession seems to be what God wills for all his people, i.e., we are called to intercede for others. No wonder Jesus is currently sitting at the right hand of God the Father interceding for us. Despite Israel's sin of idolatry, God's grace covered them and He forgave them. Grace is the inspiring and eternal theme in the story of the Golden Calf, and it is the theme of God's salvation. By extension, Kenneth Harris points to another important trajectory of the story that "While illustrating the unfaithfulness of many people, the account highlights the faithful maturing of Moses as a leader and shows him bearing aspects of God's character."[40] Moses has learned to be transformed by the grace of God throughout the time he has been with the LORD since Exodus 3. By this time, Moses had understood that the holy God who demands holiness is also a merciful God who forgives, even though our sins be as red as scarlet.[41]

A critical and reflective reading of Exodus 34:5–8 recounts a dialogue between God and Moses following the infamous golden calf scandal. This dialogue is Moses' intercession for the people

40. Kenneth Harris, "Exodus" 197.

41. Cf Isaiah 1:18.

of Israel. In the intercessory dialogue, Moses sought an assurance from God and requested him to show him his glory. God responded by allowing Moses to see his back and went further to pronounce his holy character:

> The LORD, the LORD God, merciful and gracious, long-suffering, and abounding in goodness and truth, keeping mercy for thousands, forgiving iniquity and transgression and sin, and by no means clearing the guilty, visiting the iniquity of the fathers upon the children and the children's children to the third and the fourth generation.[42]

When God proclaimed his holy character to Moses, Moses made haste and bowed his head toward the earth, and worshiped.[43] Moses' response is what we all are urged to do as believers in Africa, i.e., reverently worshipping and serving Yahweh, for him alone is worthy of worship. Therefore, Moses' posture in honoring and worshiping God shows us how we should live our life even as we make intercession for others. Moses had a unique stature among humans, he possessed superhuman traits as Deut 34:10–12 portrays him:

> Since then, no prophet has arisen in Israel like Moses, whom the LORD knew face to face, who did all those miraculous signs and wonders the LORD sent him to do in Egypt—to Pharaoh and to all his officials and to his whole land. For no one has ever shown the mighty power or performed the awesome deeds that Moses did in the sight of all Israel.

Such is the assessment of the caliber of a man that Moses was, i.e., powerful and mighty in miraculous deeds as the Servant of the LORD. Such miraculous deeds could be nothing but his humble intercession for God's people.

Therefore, through Moses' walk and experience with God since his call in Exodus 3, Moses had come to understand the character of Yahweh, the God of Israel's forefather as a holy and

42. Exodus 34: 6–7.
43. Exodus 34:8.

mighty God and that idolatry cannot coexist with him because He cannot be identified with any of the material world whether seen or unseen, corporeal or incorporeal. Through his walk, Moses became aware that Yahweh is a gracious and merciful God, hence his appeal for God to forgive his people despite their immediate forgetfulness of his gracious deliverance and salvation.

CONCLUDING STATEMENTS ON THE PERSON AND CHARACTER OF MOSES

While the Exodus events are wrapped up around the person of Moses and the work of Yahweh, Moses is the central figure in the Pentateuch from Exodus to Deuteronomy. Critical reading and reflection of the material in these books show that Moses is understood as:

1. A royal son who was raised in the palaces of the Pharaoh;

2. A shepherd man who first shepherded his father-in-law, Jethro's flock in Midian, and later shepherded God's people, the Israelites;

3. The founder of Israelite religion, Judaism gave th Israelites the Law for their personal, community and national governance;

4. The founder of Israelite nation which was officially constituted at Mount Sinai when God made a covenant with Israel and sanctified it as his holy nation;

5. The organizer of the tribal system's work and worship;

6. The founder and organizer of the judicial system of Israel;

7. The charismatic leader who knew Yahweh face to face, to the point of challenging (as he interceded for Israel) God's decision, albeit in a humble manner.

However, despite all these facts being true, Moses is depicted as the mediator of Yahweh and the people of Israel, largely seen as the intercessor between God and the people, i.e., when the people sin before God—persistent breaking of the covenant. Moses is the intercessor—one who prays, pleads, and stands in the gap between sinful Israel and faithful/righteous/holy God. Talking of intercessory role of Moses, as a prophet, this one was one of his major accomplishments. He defended the people before Yahweh. A reflective narrative on this merits our attention at this point. This is one of the critical things that can be said about Moses.

Yahweh's statement in Exodus 14:12, "I would fain strike them with pestilence and disown them, let me make of you a nation. . ." could be a statement which is semantically equivalent to the LORD's request of Moses to intercede. By asking Moses not to intercede implies that God as much as admits that prophetic intercession is effective. And Moses had at this time understood that Yahweh is a gracious God and would forgive. At the same time, God seems to be hinting to Moses—perhaps even testing him that he should intercede if he wants to save Israel. The Psalmist, citing a striking image from Ezekiel 22:30, pays this tribute to Moses' intercessory achievement: "He would have destroyed them, had not Moses, his chosen one, stood in the breach in front of them, to keep his wrath from destroying them" (Psalm 106:23). The book of Numbers confirms that Moses interceded for his people at every turn and thereby assuaged the divine wrath.[44]

The intercessory posture of Moses could certainly be argued from the point that he was the most humble person in the face of the earth (Numbers 12:3). Moses brushes aside Joshua's warning that that the prophesying of Eldad and Medad is a threat to his leadership: "Are you jealousy for me? I would like all of the Lord's people be prophets" (Numbers 11:29). All this proves that Moses' had at this time reached new heights of spiritual maturity. His concerns were not self-interests but other people's interests. This is the maturity that God wants, praying for others, interceding for them, blessing them even if they harm us. No wonder Jesus urges us to even love our enemies (Matthew 5:43–48). And Paul urges us to consider other people's interests and not only ours (Philippians 2: 4–9). The person and character of Moses is the posture we all must emulate as God's children in every way.

44. See Numbers 11:2; 12: 13; 14: 13–20; 16:22; 21:7.

4

DAVID: A MAN AFTER GOD'S OWN HEART[1]

INTRODUCTION

LIKE MOSES AND ABRAHAM before him, David is described as one of the greatest figures in the history of the nation of Israel. Scripturally, he ranks in the traditions of the patriarchs: Abraham, Isaac, and Jacob, Moses, and the great prophets. Despite his rank with these great personalities in the history of Israel, biblical tradition shows that he towers them all to some extent due to the fact that he founded the great Davidic empire whose capital, Jerusalem is not a mere city, past, present and future. Rather, it is a city whose owner is Yahweh, the God of Israel. Perhaps another reason is the very fact that the God describes David as a man after his own heart in the book of 1 Samuel. This chapter therefore discusses the person and character of David. It focuses on the significance of David in the whole panorama of the Bible, thereby examining the identity of David, his person, character and reign with a leaning of what such a story has to offer to Christian academy and the Church for

1. See 1 Samuel 13:14.

their appropriation in their own contemporary situations. The chapter does all this through a personal analysis and reflection of the scriptures and other available sources that talk about David's life and character. A brief focus on the Davidic covenant will be a very interesting aspect in this chapter, as the covenant describes David's relationship with Yahweh, the God of his forefathers and his relationship to the future and glorious Kingdom of God.

When God had called a people, and adopted them into his very possession, Judah became his sanctuary and Israel his dominion.[2] When God called Israel at the foot of Mount Sinai, he wanted them to be a kingdom of priests who would serve Him with all their hearts.[3] However, it must be noted that God's calling for Israel did not really begin on Mount Sinai. Rather, it was in Abraham in Genesis as we have already noted in chapter 2. It took about four hundred years after Israel had settled in the Promised Land before it had a strong monarch under David as its leader. Those 400 years followed Israel's leaderless-ness after Joshua, when everyone did what was pleasing in their eyes,[4] and God could raise up judges to lead them into battles against their enemies.[5] Between the settlement in Canaan and David's coming on the throne of Israel, Israel was ruled by Judges of whom the last was Samuel who anointed Saul to be Israel's first king and David as Israel's second king.

In order to accomplish its objective of telling the story of David, this chapter discusses the life of David beginning with a sketchy portrayal of his father and mother, an analysis which shows the unboggable grace of God under play in the life of David, for David, to David and for the entire nation of Israel and perhaps for the emergency of the world's Savior, the Son of God, the Son of David. Then it is followed by an overview of the Davidic Covenant in 2 Samuel 7:5–16; 18–29. Therefore, a thorough analysis of the person and character of David, a very important part of this chapter in the development of the Davidic Covenant that God

2. See Psalm 114: 1–2.
3. See Exodus 19:6 and Revelation 5:10; 20:6.
4. See Judges 21:25.
5. See Judges 2:16.

established with him is discussed which includes David's carrying out of a census—which ultimately takes us to his intercession for the people when there was disaster on the nation. This is finally followed by a conclusion in which some recommendations and important theological conclusive statements are made.

DAVID'S FATHER AND MOTHER[6]

Before we go into discussion of the Davidic covenant, which shows what kind of a man he was before God, not much is talked about David himself as a person, except that he was a son of Jesse. It is to this that I would like to draw attention as who David really was—his family background in which a knowledge of his father as well as his mother is paramount so as to establish the concrete grounds upon which God's grace of election, adoption and salvation is founded and make some responsible and pertinent theological inferences.

It must be admitted from the onset that writing something about David's mother is a difficulty venture as not much has been put in writing concerning this. So, the worthy of the material in this discussion comes from my own personal analysis and reflection of the passages on David's life and a great deal from the rare writing of David Searle's studies. Reading through the books of Samuel, Kings, and Chronicles, it becomes a little hazy over the complex relationships between some of the characters who feature in David's narratives. There are, for example, the three sons of Zeruiah: Joab, Abishai and Asahel in 2 Samuel 2:18; 1 Chronicles 2:16b. And there is Amasa, the son of Abigail, Zeruiah's sister, whom Absalom, when he rebelled, appointed him general commander of the army in place in Joab (2 Samuel 17:25; 19:3; 1 Chronicles 2:17). And these four men, were apparently David's nephews as their mothers, Zeruiah and Abigail were David's sisters (1 Chronicles 2:16a). So far, so good, as David's mighty men,

6. I am indebted to David Searle, "Who is David's Mother," *Rutherford Journal of Church and Ministry* (Claremont, Edinburg: Rutherford House, 1994), 16–17.

captains of his victorious armies were his nephews, sons of his two sisters mentioned in scriptures. But the complications begin when we read that Abigail was also a daughter of Nahash (presumably) the Ammonite king. The scriptures read as follows:

> Absalom had appointed Amasa over the army in place on Joab. Amasa was the son of Jether, an Ishmaelite who had married Abigail, the daughter of Nahash and sister of Zeruiah the mother of Joab.[7]

With this what then was David's relationship with Nahash, especially in this context that his sister Abigail was the daughter of Nahash?[8]

David Searle in his attempt to understand this complexity talked to his Israeli friend Jack about the problem of David's relationship with Nahash. Jack was a Jew, born and raised in Israel, a Jew who knows the Old Testament Scripture as well, if not better than most European and American theologians. David suggested to him that there were some strands of evidence that David's mother had been either a concubine or wife of Nahash the Ammonite, and his friend Jack agreed. David Searle tells Jack that 'our European Old Testament scholars say that 2 Samuel 17:25 is probably a corrupt text. What do the present-day rabbis say to that?'[9] Jack told him that they didn't like the suggestion at all that David had Ammonite links, and they got out with it the same way as European scholars by arguing that the original Hebrew had been changed at some point. They preferred to remove the name of Nahash altogether from 2 Samuel 17:25.[10]

Searle's pointing out of other strands of the narrative which might be understood as pointing to some link between Nahash and David's mother is worthy consideration. These strands are Searle's arguments for David's and Nahash's relationship. First, is the issue of feud. Critical biblical reading shows that there is the

---

7. 2 Samuel 17:25.

8. David Searle, "Who is David's Mother," 16.

9. David Searle, "Who is David's Mother," 16.

10. David Searle, "Who is David's Mothers," 16.

character of the nephews, as men who were more warlike and bloodthirsty than the Hebrew usually was. David himself shared that propensity for war, even excelling his nephews in military genius and prowess, but he also had a gentle and peace-loving side to his character. "What do you and I have in common, you sons of Zeruiah?"[11] These cousins of David were deeply into feuds, carrying grudges for years until they at last found the opportunity to avenge a brother's death. David himself deplored this cruel feuding in 2 Samuel 2:18–28; 3:22–39. His lament for Abner, a victim of the feud, (though no fault of his own—Abner had killed Asahel in self-defense), is very moving. The contrast between David and his nephews is brought out by the final words of the account of the assassination: "These sons of Zeruiah are too strong for me. May the LORD repay the evildoer according to his evil deeds" (2 Samuel 3:39).

Second, is the issue of Nahash's kindness to David. "In the course of time, Nahash king of the Ammonites died, and his son succeeded him as king. David thought, "I will show kindness to Hanun son of Nahash, because his father showed kindness to me" (2 Samuel 10; 1 Chronicles 19). The word used is *hesed*, covenant love.[12] The conjecture in this is that since Saul had roundly defeated Nahash as the first warlike act of his reign (1 Samuel 11), when David became a fugitive in the area of Adullam (in Ammonite territory), he and Nahash made common cause on account of their hunted or hostiled by Saul, King of Israel. David, therefore, must have made the occasional visit to Ammonite territory where he was kindly received by Nahash, hence *hesed*. However, the problem with that conjecture is that there is no account of any such relationship developing between David and Nahash. Why the silence? Some relationship between these two was undoubtedly there. Could it be that the relationship was one that the chroniclers preferred to avoid, because it was a link through

11. David angrily asked Abishai who wanted to kill Shimei in cold blood (2 Samuel 19:21–23).

12. David Searle, "Who is David's Mother," 16.

David's mother who had at some time in her younger days been a member of Nahash's harem?[13]

Third, David ignored by his father. Consider the rather surprising narrative of the anointing of David by Samuel (1 Samuel 16) when Samuel calls for Jesse's sons. We have traditionally understood Jesse's ignoring of David to have been on account on his age. The other brothers were fully grown men, three of them in Saul's army. David was still a youth, tending the flock of his father, and whose role in the war with the Philistines was merely to take some supplies to his three brothers (1 Samuel 17).

Now might there be another reason why Jesse passed over David or ignored David when Samuel called for his sons? There might be for sure. There was apparently reluctance on Jesse's part because he was painfully aware that this youngest son of his was the result of an indiscretion on his part, bringing a woman into his family who had had an earlier liaison or affair with a foreign king who had been hostile to Israel?[14] Questions would be, might that make David something of an oddity (peculiar) in the family? Might it throw some light on the antagonism of his oldest brother Eliab toward him when he saw him in the army camp, and called him 'conceited' and 'wicked' (1 Samuel 17:28). Eliab used strong language, and we are told that he burned with anger. Is this yet another piece of a jigsaw puzzle whose pieces come together to show a shepherd boy who was rather different from his brothers, because his mother was different? And the jealous was already there because David's mother was so different from Jesse's other wife or wives, being striking beautiful and gifted (which is why she had been a partner of the Ammonite king, and of course gave birth to David who was very handsome as compared to his brothers)? And mighty that be the reason behind David's handsomeness?[15] In the narratives of these verses, we read,

---

13. David Searle, "Who is David's Mother," 16.
14. David Searle, "Who is David's Mother," 16.
15. David Searle, "Who is David's Mother," 16.

So he sent and had him brought in. He was ruddy, with a
fine appearance and handsome features. Then the LORD
said, 'Rise and anoint him; he is the one. So Samuel
took the horn of oil and anointed him in the presence
of his brothers, and from that day on the Spirit of the
LORD came upon David in power, Samuel then went to
Ramah.[16]

There might indeed be some reason (s) as to why Jesse ignored
David. A motif that we will consider when we try to understand
God's grace and its out-workings later in the chapter.

Fourth, is the issue of David's unique gifts. This is the last
piece of the puzzle. There is no doubt about this, David, the youngest son of Jesse was a remarkable man. David's gifts were quite out-
standing and marvellous. He was a theologian, a poet, a shepherd,
a fighter, a general, a leader and musician, with a love for exquisite
women into the bargain.[17] Could a vital element in his make-up
be that David's mother was not the mother of David's seven brothers? A further critical question is: Is one of the greatest messages
of David's life something that we have missed for generations,
simply because ancient chroniclers did not want to admit openly
that his very existence was the result of an old man's, i.e., Jesse's
[foolish] liaison with a dubious woman who had at some point in
time been involved in sensual affairs with a non-Israelite? What
might that message be? Critically and simply put: God delights to
take up the rejects of society, the pieces of shrapnel from wrecked
relationships, and transform them by his grace into instruments of
his glory. David Searle wonders whether David's words in Psalm
51:5 regarding his conception "in sinfulness" might not refer to
his fathers' sinful relationship with his mother.[18] In all this, Searle
argues that "if David's mother was a Hebrew woman whose reputation was distinctly tarnished by her past sexual associations, but
whom Jesse took in, then we have an instance of the hand of God

16. 1 Samuel 16:12–13.

17. More on this in the ensuing section when I discuss the person and
character of David.

18. David Searle, "Who is David's Mother," 17.

at work that ought to be a massive encouragement to believers and non-believers alike on at least two levels:"[19]

First, that God can turn the unhappiest and most unadvised of events to his own purposes. Second, those whose past has been marred by the jagged fragments of human folly can be redeemed and transformed to become men and women after God's own heart. This is, after all, the very center and soul of the Story of Salvation, which is God's business of turning all of us, the descendants of Adam and Eve to be after God's own heart, so that He can lavish his love on all of us.[20] Commenting on the issue observed and raised by Searle, Desmond Alexander states that "it is possible the observations in that article are correct. A reasonable case is presented, though on the basis of the arguments put forward, it is not conclusive. Other possibilities exit. It is possible that only Zeruiah and Abigail are the children of unnamed wife or concubine of Nahash. It is also possible that Jesse may have been known as Nahash."[21] However, the argument by Alexander has a toll order to be accepted. Surely, Jesse might or could not be Nahash.

Thus far, the identity of David's mother has been explored albeit with no conclusive statement. His father was Jesse and his unnamed mother might be what we have discussed above, i.e., one who at one point associated herself with Nahash, king of Ammonites. However, with all this in mind, the Yahweh, the God revealed in the Bible is a gracious, loving and merciful God who redeems people from the bondage of slave to Satan and sin into his wonderful and glorious Kingdom of light and of His Son Jesus Christ. He is the God who turns and uplifts the lowly for his own glory. Yahweh indeed a God whom the apostle Paul states that God uses the base things, the unwise, the weak, the despised and the unknown to confound the wise.[22]

19. David Searle, "Who is David's Mother," 17. These constitute great theological motifs if David could be described as 'almost a bastard.'

20. See 1 John 3:1–3.

21. Desmond Alexander, *The Rutherford Journal of Church and Ministry*, 17.

22. See 1 Cor. 1:26–29.

GOD'S COVENANT WITH DAVID
(2 SAMUEL 7:5–16; 18–29)

We read that King David, victorious over his enemies on all sides, said to the prophet Nathan, "See now, I dwell in a house of cedar, but the ark of God dwells within the tent curtains" (2 Samuel 7:2). But the word of God given to Nathan to tell David says,

> Go and say to My servant David, 'Thus says the LORD, Are you the one who should build me a house to dwell in? For I have not dwelt in a house since the day I brought up the sons of Israel from Egypt, even to this day; but I have been moving about in a tent, even in a tabernacle. Wherever I have gone with all the sons of Israel, did I speak a word with one of the tribes of Israel, which I commanded to shepherd my people saying, 'why have you not built Me a house of cedar?[23]

Just like Moses, God's calls David, 'My Servant.' The divine word proceeds to proclaim that instead of David building a house for God, it would be God who 'will make a house for you [David]' (verse 11), and your house and your kingdom shall endure before Me forever; your throne shall be established forever (verse 16).

The Davidic covenant also knows as Zion covenant was unconditional, grounded only in God's firm and gracious purpose. However, in as much as it was an unconditional covenant, our God who is the God of synergism who likes working with his people and as such, there are some conditionalities that were to be met by David and his descendants if what God had promised was to be fully realized.[24] For example, God's making a covenant with David was due to His own faithfulness and also due to David's total devotion to God as Israel' king and the LORD's anointed vassal had come to be a special expression. The Davidic Covenant was a Royal Grant type of covenant and thus unconditional and it found

---

23. 2 Samuel 7.5–7; See also Michael Lodahl, *The Story of God*, 114.

24. See 2 Kings 2:1–4; 2 Kings 3:14; 2 Kings 6:12–13. The condition was obedience and total devotion on the part of David's descendants.

its ultimate fulfilment in the kingship of Jesus Christ who was born of the tribe of Judah and of the house of David.[25]

We need not forget that God's covenant with David follows God's covenant with Abraham where God made a covenant with Abraham in Genesis 15, when he made Abraham to sleep so that he could pass alone between the covenant meal, demonstrating that it is Him and Him alone who would fulfil the promises made to Abraham and his descendants so that indeed, "all the families on earth should be blessed."[26] So whatever was happening in the subsequent covenants between Abrahamic and Davidic covenants, were dependent on God's faithfulness to his own word, nothing else! This understanding lies in the non-conditionality of the Davidic covenant.

God's covenant with David stands in direct continuity with the Mosaic covenant as well as the Abrahamic covenant. However, at the superficial level, the focus here is on a household rather than the entire Israelite community. But intrinsically, it concerns the entire nation of Israel as well as all the families of the earth, as the Davidic Messiah came to be the Savior of the whole world. The Davidic king was God's son who ruled Israel, God's people with whom He made a covenant as Sinai. This in some biblical theology circles is known as the *Royal Theology* which engendered the belief that the reign of the Davidic king represented God's reign over his people. Various psalms reflect this understanding of kingship.[27] Over time, the term *mashiach* came to represent the ideal Davidic king who would properly embody the just reign of God over Israel and ultimately over the whole earth.

---

25. Compare the following scriptural passages Psalm 98:30–38; Isaiah 9:1–7; Matthew 1:1; Luke 1:32–33, 69; Acts 2:30; 13:23, Romans 1:2–3; 2 Timothy 2:8; Revelation 3:7; 22:16.

26. See Genesis 12:1–3.

27. For example, see Psalms 2; 18; 20; 21; 72; 110 and 132.

THE TERMS OF THE DAVIDIC COVENANT

1. The Davidic covenant meant that God established the house of David forever—the Davidic dynasty to be established. This is what greatly influenced the Messianic Hope in Israel. A Messiah like unto David will come and conquer all Israel's enemies so that Israel as a nation will be at rest. This means that David's kingdom was to endure forever.

2. David together with his sons after him to totally devote themselves to God and do whatever God commands them and walk in his ways and do what is right in his eyes by keeping his statutes and commands.[28] This is the very thing that God wanted of Abraham's descendants when he calls Abraham: "For I have called him so that he may instruct his descendants to do righteousness and justice."[29]

3. The sign for the covenant was that one of David's sons' was always to be on the throne of his father David was in itself a sign. This was started right in the life time of David when he saw this fulfilled in his son Solomon who sat on his throne when he was still alive. However, David's son on the throne was a pointer to David's 'Greater Son' Jesus Christ who was to be on this throne forever leading and judging his people with righteousness and justice.

The Davidic tradition as viewed by Brevard Childs'[30] chief interest in the rise of the kingdom focuses without doubt on David. It is difficult to overestimate the importance for the biblical tradition of David, who rivals Moses in significance for the entire canon.[31]

28. See 2 Kings 2:1–4; 2 Kings 3:14; 2 Kings 6:12–13.

29. Genesis 18: 19.

30. In what follows here, I am indebted to Brevard Child, *Biblical Theology of the Old and New Testaments: Theological Reflection on the Christian Bible* (Minneapolis: Fortress Press, 1993), 153–154.

31. Brevard Child, *Biblical Theology of the Old and New Testaments: Theological Reflection on the Christian Bible* (Minneapolis: Fortress Press, 1993), 153–154.

However, the link between the two great covenants, Sinai and Zion, remains a continual focus for theological debate. The Deuteronomistic Writer inherited several cycles of tradition regarding David which he transmitted with little alteration. The chief cycles were his rise to power in 1 Samuel 16: 14–2 Samuel 5: 12, and the so-called succession narrative in 2 Samuel 6; 7; 9–12. In the first cycle David is portrayed as a somewhat ambiguous, but ambitious soldier who participates in various political intrigues and rivalries till by planning and good fortune he achieves leadership over the tribes in Judah. Then following the debacle of Saul's war with the Philistines, David becomes ruler of both Judah and Israel.[32] Several notable features of the tradition became the focus for great expansion and growth. First, David's choice of Jerusalem as his political capital, and also as a new center for Israel's religious tradition, was symbolized by his bringing up to the city the Ark of the (Mosaic) covenant, that ancient symbol of God's presence among his people. Jerusalem or rather Zion became increasingly not merely the City of David; but the City of God. Therefore, all the mythopoetic imagery of the heavenly abode was transferred to Zion and celebrated in countless psalms as the place of God's dwelling (Psalms 46, 48, 76, etc).[33] One only has to recall the portrayal of Zion as the highest of all mountains of the earth to which all the nations flow in universal peace (Isaiah 2:2–4; Micah 4:1–2) to see the transhistorical dimensions soon attached to Zion.[34]

Second, in the form of Nathan's prophecy (2 Samuel 7) David's kingship was not only legitimatized, but extended to his posterity as an eternal covenant (Psalms 89:30–38; 132:11ff, Isaiah

---

32. Brevard Child, *Biblical Theology of the Old and New Testaments: Theological Reflection on the Christian Bible* (Minneapolis: Fortress Press, 1993), 153–154.

33. Brevard Child, *Biblical Theology of the Old and New Testaments: Theological Reflection on the Christian Bible* (Minneapolis: Fortress Press, 1993), 153–154.

34. On the political and religious importance of Jerusalem which David fulfilled, refer to Deuteronomy 12. See also Hermann Mvula, *The Theory, Praxis and Pursuit of Constitutionalism in Democratic Malawi: An Old Testament Ethical Perspective* (Zomba: Kachere Series, 2020).

9:1–7). Reading and comparing the New Testament passages reveal all this biblical truth.[35] Childs argues that "if there had once been doubt regarding the question of monarchy, the prophetic promise once-and-for-all altered the situation dramatically. Increasingly, David's rule became a symbol of theocracy in Israel, i.e., God's rule."[36] Theocracy here means human agents leading God's people by upholding God's ethical and moral standard of justice, a value so vital to any good governance in the world. It is not the poplar mistaken notion of God's direct rule on people. Rather, in his sovereign power, God lets people make decisions and choices that will guide their nations.[37] It is rather God's transcendent sovereign power that flattens and disperses power among the people for efficiency and good governance. Christopher Wright states,

> The supreme authority is thus Yahweh himself, whose theocratic focus of power and authority in a vertical sense effectively flattens and disperses power at the horizontal level. The constitutional aspects of human authority are thus set firmly in the context of God's transcendent authority and revealed will and word.[38]

This is the meaning and notion of theocracy—God dispersing vertical sovereign power, flattening it at horizontal level for humans to govern themselves.

Indeed, it was with David that God inaugurated his righteous kingdom on earth, a kingdom which Christ came to fully inaugurate in the fullness of time and he will come to ultimately establish and consummate when he comes back. One recalls how

35. See for instance, Matthew 1:1; Luke 1:32–33, 69; Acts 2:30; 13:23, Romans 1:2–3; 2 Timothy 2;8; Revelation 3.7; 22:16.

36. Brevard Childs, *Biblical Theology of the Old and New Testaments: Theological Reflection on the Christian Bible*, 153–154.

37. See for instance, Hermann Mvula, "Toward a Theology that Responds to Governance and Political Processes in Malawi: A Biblical Perspective from the Book of Deuteronomy," in *Decolonizing the Theological Curriculum in an Online Age*, edited by Felix Nyika, Ken Ross and Hermann Mvula (Zomba: Theological Society of Malawi, 2022), 251–274.

38. Christopher Wright, *Deuteronomy* (Grand Rapids, MI: Baker Books, 1996), 203.

triumphant and hilarious Christ as the son of David and the eternal righteous King entered Jerusalem. The Bible as recorded by Matthew says,

> The crowds that went ahead of him (Jesus) and those that followed shouted: 'Hosanna to the Son of David!' 'Blessed is he who comes in the name of the Lord!' 'Hosanna in the highest!'[39]

In describing Jesus's entry into Jerusalem, on his part, Mark records:

> 'Hosanna!' 'Blessed is he who comes in the name of the Lord!' 'Blessed is the coming kingdom of our father David! 'Hosanna in the highest!'[40]

Focusing on Jesus' kingship as being that of David, Luke says,

> When they came near the place where the road goes down the Mount of Olives, the whole crowd of the disciples began joyfully to praise God in loud voices for all the miracles they had seen: 'Blessed is the king who comes in the name of the Lord! 'Peace in heaven and glory in the highest!'[41]

John describes it this way:

> The next day the great crowd that had come for the feast heard that Jesus was on his way to Jerusalem. They took palm branches and went out to meet him, shouting, 'Hosanna!' 'Blessed is he who comes in the name of the Lord!' 'Blessed is the King of Israel!' 'Do not be afraid, O Daughter of Zion; see, your king is coming, seated on a donkey's colt.'[42]

It is very interesting that all the four gospel writers recorded something about Jesus' triumphal entry into Jerusalem, the City of his father David, the City of God. It is also noteworthy that what is stake in all these gospel records is homage to Jesus, the very homage

39. Matthew 21:9.
40. Mark 11:9–10.
41. Luke 19:37–38.
42. John 12:12–13, 15.

Jews would only do before God. Why? My only quick guess and argument is that the issue of the Messianic/Davidic kingdom is very paramount to the whole economy of God's Salvation which is wrought by God in Jesus Christ, His Son, the Son of David and the Son of Abraham, Son of Adam, Son of God, as Matthew and Luke attest.

It is very interesting therefore that Luke goes all the way back to Jesus being the son of Adam, the son of God. In his genealogy Luke shows Jesus' relationship to the whole human race, a reference point on how his death on the Cross was able to bring back the entire estranged human race to God. It was to establish his righteous kingdom in people's hearts and in the world that God came in the human form, in Jesus Christ. It is through his establishment of his reign in people's hearts that God wants to do away with the satanic deeds in the world.

Therefore, in his identity of Jesus, Matthew calls Jesus Son of David, i.e., an acknowledgment of Jesus being a descendant of David and thus a king himself and a promised Messiah. Mark makes a point by putting it straight that the coming of Jesus Christ was a coming of the Davidic kingdom. For Mark, Jesus is the One who must sit on the throne of David his father. Luke identifies Jesus as king who brings peace, since to Luke Jesus fulfils the Old Testament prophecies especially those made by prophet Isaiah picking one of his very titles as "Prince of Peace." John makes a sweeping statement identifying Jesus as the King of Israel who comes to enter Jerusalem, that city of David and as such, his subjects including women should not be afraid because their King is a strong tower who protects them from all enemy attacks. This was a reminiscent of who David was and what he offered to the people of Israel—protection of all the 12 tribes of Israel from all enemies and thus security for the people of Israel.

Therefore, the so-called the idealization of David's rule reaches its height in Chronicler who omits all mention of David's murky past and focuses attention on his role as an ideal political and religious leader for Israel. This understanding of David's political and theological role had been underway long before the Chronicler's portrait. In the final chapters of 2 Samuel 21–24, one can see that David was already being portrayed as the ideal ruler of Israel, even as a type of the righteous rule of God. No wonder, every ruler of Israel/Judah was evaluated based on whether they walked 'in the ways of their father David or not.'[43]

Although it remained for the prophets to develop this tradition in a variety of ways, this accounts for the move of the later tradition to identify David's rule with that of God's. In addition, the messianic hope which was attached to David provided the basis for applying the mythopoetic language of the royal psalms to the reigning Israelite king Psalms 2, 20, 21, 45, 72 as it has already been pointed out.[44] Although the original context of these psalms was certainly foreign to Israel, the mythopoetic language could still function to express Israel's faith in the coming righteous rule of God's anointed One, David's Greater Son (Luke 1:30–33).

THE STAMINA'S DAVID'S GODLY CHARACTER: HIS INTERCESSION FOR THE PEOPLE

2 Samuel chapters 11 and 12 narrate shameful acts of King David. After David had conquered almost all of Israel's enemies, he rested. However, there were some pockets of resistance to his reign which he had to deal with yet. It was therefore during one of those battles that a bad thing happened to David. As the narrative speaks of such twin shameful act of King David, implicitly the narrative also shows the greatness of David before Yahweh, the God of Israel and her forefathers.

When David had committed adultery with Bathsheba and then eventually murdered her husband Uriah, the Hittite, God

---

43. Compare the historical narratives in Kings and Chronicles as they discuss various kings of Judah and Israel. Obviously, the key to this development certainly lies in the messianic hope of Israel whose roots are to be found in Nathan's prophecy of a righteous ruler through whom the dynasty of David would be established forever.

44. See Brevard Childs, *Biblical Theology of the Old and New Testaments: Theological Reflection on the Christian Bible*.

rebuked him through the prophet Nathan. Unlike the late king Saul of Israel before David, during the time of Prophet Samuel, who arrogantly defended his foolish actions, King David did not defend his twin evils. Instead, he had a remorseful heart and repented of his sins before God. That action was followed by the consequences of his sins which had to take him to intercede for the nation of Israel, even to the point of challenging God that if He had to punish, let God punish him not the people, because it is him who had sinned. Moses challenged God following the Golden calf debacle in Exodus by telling Him to blot him out of his book and from the face of the earth. David interceded with God to remove the plague among the people, and God listened to his prayer and commanded his angel to put the sword in its place and stop killing the people.[45] David weepingly and painfully told God to punish him and not the people, stating that it is him who has sinned and not the people. I quote this to show the intensity of his words:

> When David saw the angel who was striking down the people, he said to the LORD, "I have sinned; I, the shepherd, have done wrong. These are but sheep. What have they done? Let your hand fall on me and my family."[46]

As for the punishment, God gave David a choice of three punishments for his sin: 3 years of famine, 3 months of fleeing before his enemies, or 3 days of plague. David chose the third, and Yahweh punished Israel with a plague that killed 70,000 men from Dan in the north to Beersheba in the south. As for why God punished the whole nation for the sin of the king that is exactly the question David asks in 2 Samuel 24:17: Why, when he was the one who had sinned, did the people have to suffer? He even requested that God's hand be against him and his family only, and that God would spare the people.

So, David was described as a man after God's own heart mainly because of these events as recorded in these chapters. When he sinned, he repented. And when God's anger burned against his

---

45. See 2 Samuel 24:18–25, see also 2 Chronicles 3:1.
46. 2 Samuel 24:17.

people, David interceded for them and God relented. The intercessory role of King David, while demonstrated and manifested through his writings in the psalms, much deeper can be seen in what is recorded in the 2 Samuel 24 and 1 Chronicles 21. Psalm 51 is his personal intercession and repentance after his sin with Bathsheba and eventual killing of her husband Uriah, the Hittite. So when the LORD had inflicted pain and death on the people because of David's taking of census, David interceded and pleaded to God to remove the plague. He humbly challenged Yahweh and told him that it was him who had sinned against Him and not the people. "So the LORD sent a plague on Israel from that morning until the end of the time designated, and seventy thousands of the people from Dan to Beersheba died. When the angel stretched out his hand to destroy Jerusalem, the LORD relented concerning the disaster and said to the angel who was afflicting the people, "Enough."

When David saw the angel who was striking down the people, he said to the LORD, "I have sinned; I, the shepherd, have done wrong. These are but sheep. What have they done? Let your hand fall on me and my family." In these words, David pleads that the people may not suffer for his sin, but he is the representative of God's people, and thus they bear the consequences of his behavior, whether good or evil. David offers personally to bear the punishment of this sin, but God does not accept this offer. This however, is a worthy gesture on David's part—and it sets the pattern for his descendant Messiah, who will bear the punishment due his people. That is the cradle of David's holiness—realizing that we can be the intercessors for others. The text reads:

> And that day Gad came to David and said to him, "Go up and build an altar to the LORD on the threshing floor of Araunah the Jebusite." So David went up at the word of Gad, just as the LORD had commanded. When Araunah looked out and saw the king and his servants coming toward him, he went out and bowed facedown before the king. "Why has my lord the king come to his servant?" Araunah said. "To buy your threshing floor," David replied, "that I may build an altar to the LORD, so that the

plague upon the people may be halted." Araunah said to David, "My lord the king may take whatever seems good and offer it up. Here are the oxen for a burnt offering and the threshing sledges and ox yokes for the wood. O king, Araunah gives all these to the king." He also said to the king, "May the LORD your God accept you." "No," replied the king, "I insist on paying a price, for I will not offer to the LORD my God burnt offerings that cost me nothing." So David bought the threshing floor and the oxen for fifty shekels of silver. And there he built an altar to the LORD and offered burnt offerings and peace offerings. Then the LORD answered the prayers on behalf of the land, and the plague upon Israel was halted.[47]

Then the LORD answered David's intercessory prayers on behalf of the people. And the plague was halted.

David was a man after God's own heart. Although He was not perfect, just as many of us are, his personal life and holy character pointed to Jesus the ultimate anointed One—the coming Messiah. Therefore three cardinal lessons from the story of David—from being a shepherd boy to the King of Israel could be of great interest for us Christians to emulate. These are as follows:[48]

God Values Small and What Seems to be Insignificant

When Jesse lined-up his sons, the older more advanced seemingly significant and experienced sons were not the ones that God chose. Even Samuel thought one of the elder sons of Jesse would be God's choice because according to Samuel and Jesse himself, they were likely more gifted in leadership and probably had more experience. However, God chose the youngest and the least experienced. Indeed, God places a premium on small and insignificant. He tells Samuel the following: "But the LORD said to Samuel, "Do not consider his appearance or his height, for I have rejected him.

47. 1 Chronicles 21:18–30.

48. See Becky Harling, "3 Truths We Learn about God from Samuel Anointing David" (Samuel Anoints David Bible Story and 3 Important Lessons (crosswalk.com) (accessed 24 March 2023).

The LORD does not look at the things people look at. People look at the outward appearance, but the LORD looks at the heart."[49]

Therefore, the next time we feel our faith is insignificant or our talents and gifts are inadequate, we must consider Samuel anointing David. Although he was the youngest and seemingly the most insignificant, before Samuel, before Jesse and even before his brothers, when yielded to God David became one of the greatest and mightiest of all Israel's kings. As Christians, we must position ourselves and place our little faith in God's hands and watch how He maximizes and expands it for His glory as He allows us to serve Him.

God Not Only Calls, He also Empowers Mightily

In the Bible, oil is symbolic of the Holy Spirit. It is the Holy Spirit who consecrates us, sanctifies us, sets us apart, equips and empowers us to do the will of God the Father. In the Old Testament, kings and priests were anointed with oil to symbolize sanctification, setting apart and empowerment of the Holy Spirit to do God's work. When Samuel took his horn of oil and anointed David to be the future king of Israel, it was symbolic of the holy calling God was placing on David's life. It also symbolized the fact that the Holy Spirit would empower him to do the task that God had called him to do.

In our walk with God, He God will sometimes call us to seemingly hard and impossible tasks. It could be stepping into a leadership position for which we may feel ill equipped or inexperienced. We should not be worried, God often calls his people to tasks, responsibilities, and roles beyond their natural abilities. In such situations, feelings of inability, powerlessness and inadequacy can overwhelm and at times even traumatize us. However, we must always remember that what God calls us to do, He empowers, enables, and ennobles us to do. Just as Samuel was sent by God to anoint David with oil, to symbolize the power and presence of the Holy Spirit, so He empowers us with the Holy Spirit in order to assist us to accomplish the duties He has called us to do.

49. 1 Samuel 16:7.

God Seems Never to be in Haste

David was anointed to be the king of Israel when a teenager. But he waited many years to actually become a king. It is believed that David was anointed when he was 17 years old and he became the king 13 years later. His years of waiting were very crucial to David's multifaceted growth and development. Critical reading of the Bible shows that God is always patient and that He accomplishes what He has planned and what concerns us according to His eternal timetable. In the event of our waiting for God to do what He promised and He had planned to do, He uses such waiting time to develop our character as He sets the stage for His perfect plan and accomplishments. If David had become king as soon as Samuel anointed him at his age of 17, he might have made many foolish decisions and choices. After his being anointed, God was working in David's life, shaping him in the character of His yet revealed Son Jesus Christ, and setting the stage for His divine plan and exploits for David that would follow not less than 40 years later.

Therefore, learning to wait for God's timing in accomplishing His plans for our lives and those whom He has entrusted in our care, we just have to simply be enjoying His presence as He nurtures us in our maturing process. We should not be worried or be impatient in the process. The Bible urges us to be patient.[50] Consequently, as God's children, next time we feel like God is taking forever to fulfill His promises for our lives, we should be stopping and begin to reflect on His good purpose for our life. In the process, we learn how God shapes our character. So, Becky Hurling asks, "how is God shaping our character? How might He be setting the stage for the perfect fulfillment of His plan? How can you cooperate with His timing?"[51] These are crucial questions we must consider every time of our life in this world. So David's life

---

50. Cf Isaiah 40:31; see also Psalms 27:14; Lamentations 3:25.

51. Becky Harling, "3 Truths We Learn about God from Samuel Anointing David" (*Samuel Anoints David Bible Story and 3 Important Lessons* (crosswalk. com) (accessed 24 March 2023).

teaches us more of waiting on God as He works in us to will and to do what pleases Him, rather than strictly focusing on ourselves:

> Therefore, my beloved, as you have always obeyed, not as in my presence only, but now much more in my absence, work out your own salvation with fear and trembling; for it is God who works in you both to will and to do for *His* good pleasure. Do all things without complaining and disputing, that you may become blameless and harmless, children of God without fault in the midst of a crooked and perverse generation, among whom you shine as lights in the world, holding fast the word of life. . ..[52]

This settles it perfectly well. When God seems to be taking longer time than expected, He is working in us and for us for His own good pleasure. We should do everything without complaining so that we may become blameless and harmless, children of God without fault in the midst of crooked and perverse generation. The reason we should not be complaining when God it taking His time, is given: so that we may become blameless (holy) in this crooked and perverse generation.

EXCURSUS: THE PERSON AND CHARACTER OF DAVID AND THE EFFICACY OF HIS GREAT LEADERSHIP

The analysis of the person and character of David is very important in the development of the Davidic Covenant. This section is mainly out of my own personal critical analysis and reflection of how David is portrayed in the Bible. In the Bible the character of David, son of Jesse is portrayed in the following manner:

---

52. See Philippians 2:13–14.

A Shepherd

David was a shepherd boy of his father Jesse's flock. The Bible shows that as a shepherd, David was a very good shepherd who defended his flock from any kind of harm and attack even though he was young (1 Samuel 17:34). Archeological history reveals that the Ancient Near East was infested with numerous ferocious wild animals such as lions, bears, jackals, leopards, plus other numerous cat family animals both big and small. David might have been a very good shepherd who would lead his flock in areas or pastures which were safe from such snares of danger. He did all this because he did not want any of his flock to be under harm or attack. Evidently, David cared so much for his flock that he never wanted any of them to be attacked or to be under any threat. If one of his flock was under attack by such ferocious animals, David defended them courageously and snatched them from such attackers while killing such a harmful animal. In 1 Samuel 17, when David visited his brothers who were with Saul in armed conflict with the Philistines, David told Saul his Curriculum Vitae (CV) which mentions his killing the both a lion and a bear which had attacked his flock with bare hands.[53]

A Warrior

In the Bible, David is depicted as a warrior. During his time of flights and refuge from Saul, David lived with Philistines and while there, he learned iron smelting and weapons manufacturing. As a warrior, David killed Goliath, that Philistine giant and experienced soldier who hacked and terrorized the armies of Israel during their battles. David's killing of Goliath marked his beginning point in the history of a military general who later became a feared soldier with tactics and antics in military warfare.

The Philistines descended from Cyprus and were Greek in origin, and they were Israel's stubborn, formidable and feared enemies since the time of the Judges. It was only during the time

53. See 1 Samuel 17: 34–36.

when David become king that these arch-enemies were totally defeated and pushed toward the Mediterranean Sea, i.e., the Gaza strip. David's killing of Goliath marked the beginning of their subjugation toward the nation of Israel for decades and centuries. Besides Goliath, David as a warrior fought and defeated all the enemies of God's people and left Israel at rest from all the dangers from all directions.

David fought all the enemies of Israel and the whole nation of Israel rested in the Promised Land peacefully without any threat. David's early years as Israel's second king are presented with a detailed description of his conquest of the Philistines, the Moabites, the Syrians, and the Edomites (2 Samuel 8). From these nations, David received war spoils of gold, silver, and bronze, as well as annual payments of tribute. By the time of his demise, David had established what was called the Davidic Empire which extended way into his son, Solomon's reign: Davidic-Solomonic Empire. To qualify his being a man of war, as he truly was, God denied him the responsibility of building His Temple in Jerusalem, citing the reason that "he has shed much blood."[54]

A Musician (Poet, Psalmist)

The prowess of King David's posture of greatness is also seen in his being a musician, a poet and a psalmist. King David was a great musician of the 10th to 9th century BC. As a great musician with exceptional singing skills and the talents of composing the songs, David composed a lot of songs (psalms) and apparently and skillfully played a number of various musical instruments including the harp (1 Samuel 19:9-10). As a musician and composer of songs, almost half (73 of the psalms) (songs) in the book of Psalms are said to have been composed and written by David.[55] The other

54. 1 Chronicles 22:1-10.

55. See for instance, Dentan, Robert, C. "Psalms" in Bruce M. Metzger and R.E. Murphy, eds., *The New Oxford Annotated Bible*, New York: Oxford University Press, 1977; Anderson, G.W. *The Psalms, in Peak's Commentary on the Bible*, London: Routledge, First Publication in Paperback, 2001; Estes, Daniel J.

psalms were composed and written by others people, including Moses, Heman, Solomon, sons of Korah, Asaph, and many other poets during the time of king Hezekiah.

As a musician, poet and psalmist, David sung songs of praise to God, songs of wailing, of comfort, of worship, of imprecatory against his enemies, etc. Today the Church finds great treasure in the psalms/songs that David composed and sung. The Church is edified with what David composed as songs of praise, exaltation, and worship to God. David as a musician still lives with us today in our life of songs of praise to God the Father, the Son and the Spirit. These psalms are at the heart of his intercession for his people. A number of denominations in the world sing these psalms of praise to God during times of worship. And this is one of significances of the psalms—many of them composed and written by David, the poet, son of Jesse, a man after God's own heart.

A King

David was a very great king the world has ever known. He was the greatest king of the United Kingdom of Israel. Israel's covenant God chose David and his dynasty to be his royal representative and placed him in Jerusalem what becomes His own royal earthly Seat or his throne. Therefore, as a great king after God's own heart, David shepherded God's people with integrity and skillful heart (Psalm 78:70–72). David was an ideal king for Israel, a representation of the God's righteous reign in the world. As a great king he made all the kings and their kingdom in the Ancient Near East his subjects who paid tribute to him. As a king, David was God's symbol of presence on earth.

Handbook on the Wisdom Books and Psalms: Job, Psalms, Proverbs, Ecclesiastes, Song of Songs. Baker Academic: A Division of Baker Publishing Group, Grand Rapids, MI., 2005; Kselman, J.S. and Barre, M.L. "Psalms" in *NJBC*, New York: Geoffrey Chapman, 1995; McCullough, W.S. "Psalms: An Introduction," *The Interpreter's Bible in Twelve Volumes*, IV, Twenty-5th Printing, Nashville: Abingdon, 1978; Mowinckel, Sigmund, *The Psalms in Israel's Worship in Two Volumes*, trans, by D.R.A. P Thomas Nashville: Abingdon, 1962.

The story of David in the book of 2 Samuel ends with the note that "David reigned over all Israel, *doing what was just and right*[56] for all his people. Compare with what God told Abraham concerning His will/wish for his descendants in Genesis 18:19. Here God said to Abraham: "For I have chosen him so that he will direct his children and his household (Israel and Judah) after him to keep the way of the LORD by *doing what is right and just*, so that the LORD may bring about for Abraham what he has promised him." David started fulfilling to do what God had called Abraham and his descendants to do.

As a king, David started fulfilling what God had promised Abraham in Genesis chapters 15 and 17.[57] As a king, David's dynasty was to endure forever, until David's greater son (Jesus) sits on his throne. Critical reading of King David's narratives in the Bible shows that indeed as a king, David is a type of all those who would be royal priests and kings along with Jesus Christ, David's greater son and God's Son. David reigned Israel as a nation for forty years. He reigned in Hebron for seven and half years and them in Jerusalem for thirty-three years. He rested with his father and was buried in the cave of David and Solomon his son succeeded him as king in Jerusalem and sat on the throne of David fulfilling what God had spoken to David through the Prophet Nathan. It must be noted that Solomon was crowned king, and sat on David's throne and rode on David's mule, when David was still alive.[58] Consequently, combining his personality as a warrior and king, once he had become king over all Israel as portrayed in 2 Samuel 5:1–5, David:

1. Conquered the Jebusite fortress of Jebus, renamed it Jerusalem and made it his royal city—both the political and religious capital of his kingdom (2 Samuel 5:6–10);

56. 2 Samuel 8:15. Compare with 1 Chronicles 18:14.

57. Compare Genesis 17:15–16; 21.

58. See 1 Kings 1: 28–53. To ride on David's own throne was a public proclamation that Solomon's succession to the throne was sanctioned by David himself; and not usurpation of power as some of Solomon's elder brothers had done earlier.

2. Received recognition and assurance of friendship from Hiram of Tyre, king of the Phoenicians (2 Samuel 5:11–12);

3. Decisively defeated the Philistines so that their hold on Israelite territory was broken and their threat to Israel eliminated (2 Samuel 5:17–25; 8:1);

4. Defeated the Moabites and imposed his authority over them (2 Samuel 8:2);

5. Crushed the Aramean kingdoms of Hadadezer (king of Zobah), Damascus and Maacah and put them under tribute (2 Samuel 8:3–8; 10:6–19). Talmai, the Aramean king of Geshur, apparently had made peace with David while he was still reigning in Hebron and sealed the alliance by giving his daughter in marriage to David (2 Samuel 3:3; cf. 1 Chronicles 2:23);

6. Subdued Edom and incorporated it into his empire (2 Samuel 8:13–14);

7. Defeated the Ammonites and brought them into subjection (2 Samuel 12:26–31);

8. Subjugated the remaining Canaanite cities that had previously maintained their independence from Israel, such as Beth Shan, Megiddo, Taanach and Dor.

Since David had earlier crushed Amalekites (1 Samuel 30:17–18), his wars thus completed the conquest begun by Joshua some centuries earlier and secured all the borders of Israel. His empire (united Israel plus the subjugated kingdoms) reached from Ezion Geber in the eastern arm of the Red Sea to the Euphrates River. Ernest Wright argues that,

> David, Israel's greatest leader defeated the Philistines and subdued them, breaking their power forever. His gifts as a poet/musician and statesman make him, of all Israel's kings, the most beloved by his people and the most respected by his enemies.[59]

59. Ernest Wright, *Great People of the Bible and How they Lived* (Canada: The Readers Digest Association, 1974), 164.

Such was the warrior/king that David was to Israel, fulfilling what God has promised Abraham—that his descendants will cover (or have influence on) the lands as described in chapters 15 and 17 of Genesis.

A [Political] Leader

After exploits of all the conquests, David united all the twelve tribes of Israel, organized them and began to lead them as God wanted. As a leader of a great nation on earth at that time, i.e., the United Kingdom of Israel, David led Israel to its glories through political rest from all corners of the earth, economic stability, and vast splendor. He was the greatest leader Israel has ever had in its history as a nation. He is probably paralleled with Moses as far as leadership is concerned. The world of that time feared David more than any other leader.

Despite his later faults, David was the ideal leader whose leadership qualities model that of God. He strove to live by the principles of righteousness and justice which are the very foundations of God's reign. As a leader, he really rallied behind him all Israel who whole-heartedly accepted his leadership character. As a leader, having conquered nations, David was recognized by all these nations as their leader too. No wonder in David, God found the ideal representative (leader) on earth. Again, it is small wonder that all the leaders in both Israel and Judah after David were compared to David as to whether they walked in the ways of David their father or not. He became the model or yardstick of all that is great, true, just and righteous leaders.

A Theologian

Another figure or character of David is that of being a theologian. Reading the Old Testament intently one cannot but find the fact that David was indeed a theologian. As a theologian, David understood the Omni-doctrines, the Infinity of God, the Holiness

63

of God, the Spirituality of God, and the Eternity of God with their practical implications for practical life in the entire universe. David wrote and articulated most of these divine doctrines more than any other person either implicitly or explicitly in the book of Psalms as well as in the book of 1 and 2 Samuel. Through his own experience with God, he came to understand that Yahweh is the good the shepherd, with whom any sheep will not want anything because He provides all the necessities for life. Yahweh does all this because He takes them to green pastures, restores their souls, guides them into the paths of righteousness, and prepares a table for them even before their enemies, and eventually they will dwell with Him forever. David understood God to be the protector of all those who trust in Him because his experience gave him assurance that Yahweh is the strong tower and a refuge for those who are mistreated by their enemies. David understood that our lives are dependent on God alone. In times of disasters, Yahweh is our shield and protector, and deliverer.

In a number of instances David invoked God's continual presence with him if he were to succeed and continue living as a living person. During his years as a fugitive from Saul, God was teaching these divine truths about Himself and those who trust in Him. It was during those fugitive years that David understood God as only reliable source of strength and all that is. David's understanding and articulation of theology about who God is, what the world is, and who God's children are, made him realize that there is life after this present one where those who have trusted in God will live with him in glory forever. David acknowledged that true salvation is found in none other than God himself whose Son wept *Eloi, Eloi, lama sabachthani* on the Cross of Calvary to bring about reconciliation and true relationship between God and his estranged humanity on earth.[60]

60. See Matthew 27: 45–47; Mark 15: 33–35.

CONCLUSION

Thus, is the person and character of David as this chapter has demonstrated through a comprehensive discussion and analysis. David was raised by God from being a shepherd boy to a great Emperor in the ancient near eastern world. He was a mighty warrior, a valiant military general, an inspired and inspiring leader, a great theologian, and a gifted psalm writer. But the thing that impressed God the most about David was David's heart.[61] God affirmed, "I have found David the son of Jesse, a man after my heart, who will carry out all my will" (Acts 13: 22). David allowed God to mold and fashion his heart into that which would be pleasing to Him. God focused on David's character more than his physical stature. He concentrated on his integrity and not just outward appearance.

Therefore, as a brilliant shepherd, warrior, musician, king, leader and theologian, decisive and just, David transformed Israel from a weak and divided tribedom or clandom into a formidable empire. This transformation paralleled his own progress from shepherd boy to king. Throughout his life, he was loyal to the LORD and the prophets, a fact which brought him victory against his foes and forgiveness for his every human weaknesses and sins. It is thus against this backdrop that no wonder even the future Messianic king of Israel is depicted as to be David's son and not as Saul's son or Solomon's son, or any other leader of Israel, either as a United Kingdom of Israel or as divided kingdoms of Judah and Israel. And for sure, this is what David was/is, i.e., one of the greatest sons and the greatest statesman the world has had. One who was a man after the heart of God, a fact that God would want to continue having in political leaders as well as other people, i.e., "men and women after his own heart."

---

61. Rick Ezell, https://www.lifeway.com/en/articles/sermon-inner-workings-1-develop-heart-for-god (accessed on 25 March 2023).

5

KING SOLOMON:
A DARLING FOR YAHWEH[1]

INTRODUCTION

SOLOMON, HEBREW *SHLOMO*, ALSO known as Jedidiah, was, according to the Hebrew or Old Testament, a fabulous wealthy and wise king of the United Kingdom of Israel who succeeded his father, King David. Solomon is the one who built the first Temple in Jerusalem. The conventional dates of his reign are about 970–931 BC, normally given in alignment with the dates of David's reign. Solomon is revered in the Old Testament just like in the New Testament as the wisest person in the history of the nation of Israel and the world. Only to be challenged by Jesus himself who said that 'he who is greater than Solomon is here.'[2] However, in spite of his wisdom and greatness, Solomon is regarded as one who started very well but perhaps ended very badly. By the time of the end of his reign, the David-Solomonic Empire was reduced in size, as compared to how his father David had left it—having conquered

1. See 2 Samuel 12:24–25.
2. See Matthew 12: 42; Luke 11:31.

and defeated all the kingdoms of the Mediterranean world. However, despite such a sorry ending, his starting point merits our attention, as it points to what it really means to talk about intercession by holy and godly people. This will be taken from a prayer as the following describes.

KING SOLOMON: A TYPE OF JESUS CHRIST? A KING, PRIEST AND PROPHET (1 KINGS 8: 22–53)

[22] *Then Solomon stood before the altar of the Lord in front of the whole assembly of Israel, spread out his hands toward heaven* [23] *and said: "Lord, the God of Israel, there is no God like you in heaven above or on earth below—you who keep your covenant of love with your servants who continue wholeheartedly in your way.* [24] *You have kept your promise to your servant David my father; with your mouth you have promised and with your hand you have fulfilled it—as it is today.* [25] *"Now Lord, the God of Israel, keep for your servant David my father the promises you made to him when you said, 'You shall never fail to have a successor to sit before me on the throne of Israel, if only your descendants are careful in all they do to walk before me faithfully as you have done.'* [26] *And now, God of Israel, let your word that you promised your servant David my father come true.* [27] *"But will God really dwell on earth? The heavens, even the highest heaven, cannot contain you. How much less this temple I have built!* [28] *Yet give attention to your servant's prayer and his plea for mercy, Lord my God. Hear the cry and the prayer that your servant is praying in your presence this day.* [29] *May your eyes be open toward this temple night and day, this place of which you said, 'My Name shall be there,' so that you will hear the prayer your servant prays toward this place.* [30] *Hear the supplication of your servant and of your people Israel when they pray toward this place. Hear from heaven, your dwelling place, and when you hear, forgive.* [31] *"When anyone wrongs their neighbor and is required to take an oath and they come and swear the oath before your altar in this temple,* [32] *then hear from heaven and act. Judge between*

your servants, condemning the guilty by bringing down on their heads what they have done, and vindicating the innocent by treating them in accordance with their innocence. [33]*"When your people Israel have been defeated by an enemy because they have sinned against you, and when they turn back to you and give praise to your name, praying and making supplication to you in this temple,* [34]*then hear from heaven and forgive the sin of your people Israel and bring them back to the land you gave to their ancestors.* [35]*"When the heavens are shut up and there is no rain because your people have sinned against you, and when they pray toward this place and give praise to your name and turn from their sin because you have afflicted them,* [36]*then hear from heaven and forgive the sin of your servants, your people Israel. Teach them the right way to live, and send rain on the land you gave your people for an inheritance.* [37]*"When famine or plague comes to the land, or blight or mildew, locusts or grasshoppers, or when an enemy besieges them in any of their cities, whatever disaster or disease may come,* [38]*and when a prayer or plea is made by anyone among your people Israel—being aware of the afflictions of their own hearts, and spreading out their hands toward this temple—* [39]*then hear from heaven, your dwelling place. Forgive and act; deal with everyone according to all they do, since you know their hearts (for you alone know every human heart),* [40]*so that they will fear you all the time they live in the land you gave our ancestors.* [41]*"As for the foreigner who does not belong to your people Israel but has come from a distant land because of your name—* [42]*for they will hear of your great name and your mighty hand and your outstretched arm—when they come and pray toward this temple,* [43]*then hear from heaven, your dwelling place. Do whatever the foreigner asks of you, so that all the peoples of the earth may know your name and fear you, as do your own people Israel, and may know that this house I have built bears your Name.* [44]*"When your people go to war against their enemies, wherever you send them, and when they pray to the Lord toward the city you have chosen and the temple I have built for your Name,* [45]*then hear from heaven their prayer and their plea, and uphold their cause.* [46]*"When they sin against you—for there is no one who*

68

does not sin—and you become angry with them and give
them over to their enemies, who take them captive to their
own lands, far away or near; [47]*and if they have a change of*
heart in the land where they are held captive, and repent
and plead with you in the land of their captors and say,
'We have sinned, we have done wrong, we have acted wick-
edly'; [48]*and if they turn back to you with all their heart and*
soul in the land of their enemies who took them captive,
and pray to you toward the land you gave their ancestors,
toward the city you have chosen and the temple I have
built for your Name; [49] *then from heaven, your dwelling*
place, hear their prayer and their plea, and uphold their
cause. [50] *And forgive your people, who have sinned against*
you; forgive all the offenses they have committed against
you, and cause their captors to show them mercy; [51]*for they*
are your people and your inheritance, whom you brought
out of Egypt, out of that iron-smelting furnace. [52]*"May*
your eyes be open to your servant's plea and to the plea of
your people Israel, and may you listen to them whenever
they cry out to you. [53] *For you singled them out from all*
the nations of the world to be your own inheritance, just
as you declared through your servant Moses when you,
Sovereign Lord, brought our ancestors out of Egypt."

Critical reading and reflection of Solomon's Intercessory prayer
shows that there are several important issues that are contained
therein:

1. The prayer is rooted in Solomon's trust in the good and faithful character of Yahweh, the God of Israel's forefathers;

2. The intercession is rooted in Solomon's recognition of God's
   grace in establishing him as king and giving him an enduring
   kingdom that his father, David left for him;

3. The intercession demonstrates Solomon's humility, as shown
   by his description of himself as a servant, a youth, and without leadership experience;

4. The intercession is made from a self-giving perspective, as
   Solomon seeks wisdom on behalf of God's people, and not
   necessarily for his egocentrism;

5. The intercessory prayer itself begins with the desire for obedience and only then moves to issues of discernment of good and evil.

The Bible says, "Now it pleased the LORD that Solomon had requested this" (v. 10). In every crucible of petition that Solomon makes, there are repetitions of words: "from heaven your dwelling place, forgive, forgive, forgive." Solomon prayed his prayer not only for his contemporary people, but also his focus was on the future—when God's people sin, God must graciously forgive them. In other words, Solomon understood God's nature, as a forgiving God—probably unlike the gods of the other nations—who were lifeless and could not do anything.

Critical analysis shows that Solomon's prayer was indeed an intercessory prayer per excellence. Solomon looked to the future of God's people, and interceded for them.

EXPOSITION OF SOLOMON'S LIFE AND INTERCESSORY ROLE: SYNOPSIS OF SOLOMON'S INTERCESSORY PRAYER AND ITS SIGNIFICANCE—THEN AND NOW

Solomon like his father, David, and like many other heroes of faith before him—Abraham, Isaac, Jacob, Moses, was a flawed man who loved his LORD and wanted to do right by Him. He was chosen for a purpose and destiny. Solomon was considered the wisest man in history. Writing the book of Ecclesiastes, Song of Solomon and Proverbs, all of these books contain wisdom on how we are to live our lives, love one another and walk in reverence to God. Solomon was the son of David and Bathsheba, coming out of David's great indiscretion.[3] Looks like God does not hold us responsible for our father's or mother's indiscretion but sometimes he assigns us to carry on our father's work. So Solomon's legacy was to build the

---

3. Could Solomon's story be a reminiscent of his father's story as we observed in chapter 4 where we have discussed at length the identity of David's mother? Solomon's birth was out of his father, David's indiscretion just as it could be argued of Jesse's indiscretion of fathering David?

first Temple. He would complete his father's dream because David had too much blood on his hands to be worthy of the task. 1 Kings 5:4 states "But now the LORD my God has given me rest on every side; there is neither adversary nor evil occurrence." And Solomon was dedicated to doing the will of God, he had a heart for God like his father David. In 1 Kings Chapter 3 verse 9 we read about how the LORD appeared to Solomon in a dream, in the dream Solomon has a conversation with God, prayed, requesting the following from God:

> "Therefore, give to Your servant an understanding heart to judge Your people, that I may discern between good and evil. For who is able to judge this great people of Yours?" and immediately following the Lord honored his request, pleased that Solomon did not ask for riches or long life or the defeat over his enemies but that his desire was to have a wide and understanding heart. Verse 13 states "And I have also given you what you have not asked: both riches and honor, so that there shall not be anyone like you among the kings all your days."

So, the LORD filled Solomon with His wisdom, multiplied his coffers and gave him unparalleled reputation in the world. He would need all these things if he were to undertake the construction of the Temple and govern God's people well.

A prayer by King Solomon described in 1 Kings 8:22–52 is said to have occurred at the dedication of the temple of Solomon, which also became known as the wording and thinking of the prayer have much in common with the language of Deuteronomy.[4] Reviewing the passage in 1 Kings 8 as a whole, we learn at least three things:

1. We learn how to pray. We are therefore reminded to come before God humbly, with heartfelt praise and with honorable petitions.

2. We learn something about God's holy and responsive character. God is eager to answer and sincere honorable petitions.

---

4. Barnes' Notes on the Bible on 1 Kings 8, accessed 6 October 2017.

3. We learn of the necessity of being a good steward of what God has given us. We can ask God anything and He can give us. However, whether we ask for wisdom, whether we ask for intelligence, whether we ask for riches, whether we ask for influence, whether we intercede, God requires that we use all that He gives us for His glory.

As I have already said, critical reflection of Solomon's intercessory prayer shows that it looked to the future of Israel [and of other nations]. He mentions in it many things beyond repeating here. However, among the requests and petitions are intercession for deliverance, for return from captivity, which could even depict the in-gathering of the Jewish people from all the four corners of the world, culminating in the re-establishment of the modern State of Israel in 1948, back in their ancient homeland. That prayer of Solomon is so powerful that it continues to quicken God's steadfast love for Israel—the descendants of Abraham his friend. It could be argued that many prophetic oracles of Isaiah, Jeremiah, Ezekiel, Daniel and the other so-called Minor Prophets, are rooted in Solomon's intercessory prayer for God's people on return from their diasporic situations.

Also very critical to note is that this intercessory prayer of Solomon is rooted in God's goodness, grace, kindness and mercy. God's forgiveness of the sins of his people is based on his gloriousness *hesed* relationship he had committed himself to Israel's forefathers: Abraham, Isaac and Jacob. In his intercessory role, Solomon based and appealed to God's forgiveness of his people—presently, and those in future, based on His name that He caused to be in the Temple that Solomon was dedicating at that time.

Therefore, in my analysis I would not help but extrapolate that King Solomon was a type of Jesus Christ, who was a King, Priest and Prophet. Solomon functioned as a king, a priest and a prophet, the three offices that Jesus Christ functioned.[5] As a king in the tradition of his father David, Solomon led the people in

---

5. Randy Maddox, *Responsible Grace: John Wesley's Practical Theology* (Nashville, Tennessee: Kingswood Books, 1994).

worshiping God in the temple he had built and dedicated, fulfilling Moses' wish for one place of worship in Deuteronomy 12. As a priest, he led the people in offering sacrifices which he himself and the people had brought to the temple for sacrifice. As a prophet, Solomon prophesied of the people's diasporic condition because of sin and prayed for God's bringing them back to their homeland. Indeed, Solomon's intercessory prayer continues to sustain the Jewish people and us even these days—thousands of years later. Solomon's prayer galvanizes and invigorates God's graces and mercies toward his people, i.e., the people of the world. As a descendant of Abraham, from whom God would "bless all the families of the world," Solomon acts as an intermediary mediator before Jesus, the true Seed of Abraham comes on the scene to ultimately and decisively reveal God's will for the world and One who sits on the right hand of God interceding for us.[6]

In summary, this chapter in which Solomon's intercessory prayer is seen, exemplifies Solomon's holy character, posture and lifestyle. Solomon was a priest-king-prophet indeed. He understood what it means to be holy before God. He understood the priestly role of those whom Yahweh is their God, among such roles being intercession for others. He stood in the gap between God and his people—past, present, and future.

6. Romans 8:34.

6

DANIEL: GOD'S FAITHFUL PROPHET IN CAPTIVITY

INTRODUCTION

DANIEL WAS A YOUNG man of Jewish nobility taken into captivity by Nebuchadnezzar in the third year of Jehoiakim and he was renamed Belteshazzar in Babylon. This means that Daniel was among the aristocratic people who were carried by the Babylonians in 697 BC when Nebuchadnezzar and his army torpedoed Jerusalem and carried its royalty and other well-to-do people into captivity. By the time Daniel and others were carried out, he was a young man probably in his 20s. Prophet Daniel was trained in the king's court and then elevated to a high rank in the Babylonian and Persian kingdoms. While in Babylon, Daniel was known for wisdom, integrity, and faithfulness to God. Daniel means "God is my judge," or "judge of God," or "my God is judge" in Hebrew. However, the Babylonians **who captured him from Judah wanted to wipe out any identification with his past, so they renamed him Belteshazzar, which means "may [god] protect his life."** Ironically, and indeed, Yahweh, the God of Daniel's people, protected Daniel's life through and through until he died in his old age, probably between 80 and 85 years.[1] Some sources say that he died at the age of 95. This is based on the fact that he lived between 457–362 BCE.[2]

Daniel was a prophet who always put God first. Daniel the prophet was only a teenager when introduced in the book of Daniel and was an old man at the close of the book, yet never once in his life did his faith **in God waver.** Daniel became a skilled government administrator, excelling at whatever tasks were assigned to him. His court career lasted nearly 80 years. Daniel was first and foremost a servant of God, a prophet who set an example to God's people on how to live a holy life. He survived the lion's den because of his faith in God. Daniel also predicted the future triumph of the Messianic kingdom in chapters 7 to 12 of his book. Daniel adapted well to the foreign environment of his captors while keeping his own ethical and moral values and integrity. He learned quickly. By being fair and honest in his dealings, he gained the respect of kings.

As a paradigm of spiritual resilience, Daniel displayed genuine self-sacrifice in the face of immense adversity, and holding onto his beliefs and religious practice despite the isolation of exile. Notwithstanding the spiritual darkness that enveloped him, Daniel personally retained a high level of Divine consciousness and aligned his conduct with its sacred values. He served as a shining example of genuine devotion to God for all his Jewish brethren. He is an example of all those who might find themselves serving in political positions. He interceded for his Jewish community both in exile and those in Judah.

DANIEL'S PRAYER 9

In the first year of Darius son of Xerxes (a Mede by descent), who was made ruler over the Babylonian kingdom— [2] in the first year of his reign, I, Daniel, understood

1. See "How old was Daniel in the Bible?—Sage-Advices" (accessed 25 March 2023).

2. Avrohom Bergstein, *Daniel the Prophet of the Bible, His Life and Accomplishments*—Chabad.org (accessed 25 March 2023).

from the Scriptures, according to the word of the Lord given to Jeremiah the prophet, that the desolation of Jerusalem would last seventy years. [3] *So I turned to the Lord God and pleaded with him in prayer and petition, in fasting, and in sackcloth and ashes.* [4] *I prayed to the Lord my God and confessed: "Lord, the great and awesome God, who keeps his covenant of love with those who love him and keep his commandments,* [5] *we have sinned and done wrong. We have been wicked and have rebelled; we have turned away from your commands and laws.* [6] *We have not listened to your servants the prophets, who spoke in your name to our kings, our princes and our ancestors, and to all the people of the land.* [7] *"Lord, you are righteous, but this day we are covered with shame—the people of Judah and the inhabitants of Jerusalem and all Israel, both near and far, in all the countries where you have scattered us because of our unfaithfulness to you.* [8] *We and our kings, our princes and our ancestors are covered with shame, Lord, because we have sinned against you.* [9] *The Lord our God is merciful and forgiving, even though we have rebelled against him;* [10] *we have not obeyed the Lord our God or kept the laws he gave us through his servants the prophets.* [11] *All Israel has transgressed your law and turned away, refusing to obey you. "Therefore, the curses and sworn judgments written in the Law of Moses, the servant of God, have been poured out on us, because we have sinned against you.* [12] *You have fulfilled the words spoken against us and against our rulers by bringing on us great disaster. Under the whole heaven nothing has ever been done like what has been done to Jerusalem.* [13] *Just as it is written in the Law of Moses, all this disaster has come on us, yet we have not sought the favor of the Lord our God by turning from our sins and giving attention to your truth.* [14] *The Lord did not hesitate to bring the disaster on us, for the Lord our God is righteous in everything he does; yet we have not obeyed him.* [1] *"Now, Lord our God, who brought your people out of Egypt with a mighty hand and who made for yourself a name that endures to this day, we have sinned, we have done wrong.* [16] *Lord, in keeping with all your righteous acts, turn away your anger and your wrath from Jerusalem, your city, your holy hill. Our sins and the iniquities of our ancestors have made Jerusalem and your people an object of scorn to all those around us. [17] "Now, our God, hear the prayers and petitions of your servant. For your sake, Lord, look with favor on your desolate sanctuary. [18] Give ear, our God, and hear; open your eyes and see the desolation of the city that bears your Name. We do not make requests of you because we are righteous, but because of your great mercy. [19] Lord, listen! Lord, forgive! Lord, hear and act! For your sake, my God, do not delay, because your city and your people bear your Name."*

There are many different kinds of prayers in the Bible. There are prayers of thanksgiving, prayers of praise, prayers of petition, and prayers of intercession. But there are a few prayers that are really prayers of intercessory which are confessional in nature. It can be argued that as we really mature in God's grace, it should be becoming nature in our lives to be offering intercessory prayers to God for his saving and sanctifying graces to reach out to the unsaved in the world. There are two types of confessional prayers. The first is a personal confession for personal sin, and the greatest example of that is Psalm 51, which is a heart-throbbing confession offered by King David after he had sinned in his affair with Bathsheba and the murder of her husband Uriah. But there is also corporate/communal confession, and perhaps the greatest illustration of that is here in Daniel 9. When one studies the character of Daniel in the Bible, one finds that he is one of the only men in Scripture about whom nothing bad is ever said. That does not mean he was sinless, but he never did anything that brought reproach to the name of the LORD. His life was a remarkable display of faith, prayer, devotion, holiness, steadiness and maturity. And yet, here he is, composing one of the most powerful prayers of intercession" personal and national confession in the Bible. He was confessing the sins of the Jewish people and interceding for them so that God would forgive them and remember their sins no more.

The prayer of Daniel could be born deep within our soul, erupts through our heart, and pours out on our lips, words created by and infused with the Spirit of God. It is really not an everyday type of prayer, but it is one that mature Christians ought to be exemplifying. Intercessory prayer is one that is birthed under pressure and where the individual person requests God's intervention in their situation and the situation of others. Analysis of Daniel's prayer Verses 4–19 shows the following:

1. Daniel's prayer of confession Verses 4–15

2. Daniel's intercessory petition Verses 16–19

These verses are the expression of Daniel's repentance and confession of sin, for himself and for his fellow people, the Jews. Daniel minimizes neither his sin nor the sin of his fellow people of the Jewish race. He uses a wide variety of expressions to describe sin in its various manifestations. In verse 5, Daniel says of Israel that they have:

1. "Sinned,"

2. "Committed iniquity,"

3. "Acted wickedly,"

4. "Rebelled,"

5. "Turned aside from God's commandments and ordinances."

In verse 6, Daniel adds that "we have not listened . . . to the prophets." In verse 7, Daniel refers to Israel's "unfaithful deeds." Indeed, Israel's bondage in Babylon was the consequence of her sin which the pre-exilic prophets up to prophet Jeremiah has warned them. Daniel's confession mirrors the words of 2 Chronicles 36:15–16. Therefore, Daniel understands Israel's Babylonian captivity as the curse which has come upon the Jews because they broke God's covenant made with them at Mount Sinai (verse 11). Israel's sins are seen in contrast to the character of God. Daniel's consciousness of his own sins, and those of his fellow-Israelites, was the result of his deep sense of the majesty of God as seen by His divine attributes. Consider his prayer:

> God is "great and awesome," who "keeps His covenant and loving-kindness" (verse 4). God is not just "righteous

in all He has done" (verse 14); "righteousness," "compassion," and "forgiveness" "belong to Him" (verses 7, 9).

For Daniel, the godly qualities of Yahweh could be listed as follows:

1. Great and awesome

2. Keeper of covenant

3. Loving-kindness

4. Righteous

5. Compassion

6. Forgiving

All these mean that despite being a transcendent God, Yahweh often comes down and offers love, kindness, compassion and forgiveness to all those who truly seek him with all their heart. Jeremiah tells us that if we seek him with all our heart, He will be found by us.[3]

It is one thing to be righteous, forgiving, and compassionate; it is quite another to own these qualities. Owning them means they can only be obtained from God. These qualities are under God's control. Indeed, Daniel's confession of sin is precisely what is required of Israel in order to be forgiven and restored.

> [40]If they confess their iniquity and the iniquity of their forefathers, in their unfaithfulness which they committed against Me, and also in their acting with hostility against Me— [41]I also was acting with hostility against them, to bring them into the land of their enemies— or if their uncircumcised heart becomes humbled so that they then make amends for their iniquity, [42]then I will remember My covenant with Jacob, and I will remember also My covenant with Isaac, and My covenant with Abraham as well, and I will remember the land.

Therefore, God's forgiveness of Israel's sins is solely a gracious offer based on God's gracious covenant He made with Israel's forefathers: Abraham, Isaac and Jacob. We are reminded of the

3. See Jeremiah 29:10–14.

maledictory enactment of the covenant in Genesis 15 where he has caused Abraham to sleep a very deep sleep so that God passed on the slain pieces of meat alone. Being God, he foreknew that if the covenant was to really depend on the children of Abraham, it would fail. So the fulfilment of the covenant that God made with Abraham to bless the whole human race, was solely dependent on him alone. It was by God's sheer grace and not any human endeavor. This is buttressed in the New Testament by what the apostle Paul says in Ephesians 2:8–10—that we are saved by God's grace alone and not anything that we have done.

ANALYSIS OF DANIEL'S PRAYER OF INTERCESSION AND PETITION: 9:16–19

[16]"O Lord, in accordance with all Thy righteous acts, let now Thine anger and Thy wrath turn away from Thy city Jerusalem, Thy holy mountain; for because of our sins and the iniquities of our fathers, Jerusalem and Thy people have become a reproach to all those around us. [17] "So now, our God, listen to the prayer of Thy servant and to his supplications, and for Thy sake, O Lord, let Thy face shine on Thy desolate sanctuary. [18]"O my God, incline Thine ear and hear! Open Thine eyes and see our desolations and the city which is called by Thy name; for we are not presenting our supplications before Thee on account of any merits of our own, but on account of Thy great compassion. [19]"O Lord, hear! O Lord, forgive! O Lord, listen and take action! For Thine own sake, O my God, do not delay, because Thy city and Thy people are called by Thy name."

We have already observed the pattern of Daniel's prayer in verses 4–15. It was confessional both personal and national and intercessory—for Israel. However, beginning from verse 16, a change is evident in Daniel's prayer. Critical reflection of Daniel's prayer shows the following things that are so crucial to Christian life and what ought to be their prayer lifestyles. We consider the following observations which summarize this change and its implications:

1. Daniel's prayer in verses 16–19 moves from the confession of verses 4–15 to intercessory. In the earlier verses of his prayer, Daniel asked for nothing. He acknowledged his sins and those of his people. He was agreeing with God's Word and the righteousness of the judgment He had brought upon the Jews through the nation of Babylon.

2. Daniel's intercessory prayer and request are in accordance with God's promises in Scripture. Daniel understood that the 70 years of captivity prophesied by Jeremiah had been fulfilled and that now Israel could be restored. Just as Daniel's confession fulfilled the Old Testament requirements for restoration, so did Daniel's intercession. Daniel asked for that which God had promised through the Law and the Prophets.

3. Daniel's intercessory prayer is God-centered. At least 19 times, reference is made to Yahweh, the God of Israel's forefather, the Sovereign God of the heavens and the earth. Prayer should always be God-centered not man-centered. Daniel focuses on God's righteousness and His purposes and glory.

4. Daniel's intercessions are made in accordance with God's just character where he acknowledged that God acted consistently with His character when He disciplined Israel by giving them over to the Babylonians. Now, Daniel appeals to God to act in accordance with His mercy and compassion, and His love for His people and His chosen race to the chosen place.

5. Daniel's request is for God to act in His own best interest and glory. An alarming tendency exists in Christian circles (often in contemporary Christian music) of thinking of God as being "there for me." The fact is we are "here for Him." He is using all creation, all mankind, for His glory. This includes both the salvation of His elect and the condemnation of the rest. Daniel's prayer is not for God to act in the way that best "meets man's needs" (as perceived by man), but rather for

God to act in His own best interest. But when God acts in His own best interest, it is always for the good of His own.[4] Daniel therefore petitions God to act for His sake (verses 17, 19). How radical would be the change in our prayer life if we petitioned God as Daniel did.

6. Daniel's request is for grace, mercy, and compassion. Daniel realizes that Israel's return, restoration, and future blessings are contingent upon God's grace and forgiveness. In this prayer and should be in all our prayers, sinners cannot ask for anything but grace and mercy. Daniel's prayer is not on the basis of any merit of their own that he beseeches God to answer (verse 18). Daniel pleaded for mercy, as any sinner should and must do.

7. Daniel's prayer is for more than what God is going to accomplish in the Jewish Babylonian captives' return to their land. In the Old Testament Law and in the Prophets, God promised to establish His eternal kingdom, a kingdom in which men would be perfectly restored, and in which righteousness would dwell.

THE APPEARANCE OF GABRIEL (9:20–23)

[20]Now while I was speaking and praying, and confessing my sin and the sin of my people Israel, and presenting my supplication before the LORD my God on behalf of the holy mountain of my God, [21] while I was still speaking in prayer, then the man Gabriel, whom I had seen in the vision previously, came to me in my extreme weariness about the time of the evening offering. [22]And he gave me instruction and talked with me, and said, "O Daniel, I have now come forth to give you insight with understanding. [23]"At the beginning of your supplications the command was issued, and I have come to tell you, for

4. See Romans 8:28.

you are highly esteemed; so give heed to the message and gain understanding of the vision."

Gabriel's appearance interrupted Daniel who was still praying. Gabriel's appearance and announcement was in answer to Daniel's prayers. Daniel's intercessory prayer resulted in Gabriel's prophetic announcement. Daniel's prayers of confession and intercession have been answered. Yahweh, the God of Israel, is a glorious, gracious and living God. He answers prayers. When prayed earnestly, honestly and confessionally, God answers.

IMPLICATIONS OF DANIEL'S INTERCESSORY PRAYER

When Daniel prayed this the kinds of prayers as observed in this chapter, Judah had been scattered for about 70 years, and they were just about ready to go back to the Promised Land. God was just about ready to release them. Daniel was concerned due to what he saw in Babylon; it discomforted him. He likely saw some of the same conditions existing in Babylon that had caused the Jews to go into captivity in the first place almost 70 years before. His fears were justified because, when Ezra and Nehemiah went back to rebuild the Temple and then the wall around Jerusalem, very few Jews went back. In fact, it was such a small number by Ezra's count that he called a fast about it.[5]

Daniel begins by establishing between him and God that he, Daniel, understood that God is faithful. He makes covenants; he keeps His covenant and fulfills them. He is a covenant-making God, covenant-keeping God, and covenant-fulfilling God. He stands by Leviticus 26 and Deuteronomy 28. When something goes out of God's mouth, it does not come back to Him empty

---

5. If Peter did write 1 Peter, the mention of "Babylon" in 5:13 is fairly reliable evidence that Peter resided at some time in the capital city (see https://www.google.com/search?q=Did+the+apostle+Peter+go+to+babylon&oq=Did+the+apostle+Peter+go+to+babylon&aqs=chrome..69i57.13158j0j7&sourcei) (accessed online on 24th May 2021). See also Bill Kochman https://www.billkochman.com/Articles/AMysterySolvedPeterBabylon.html (December 26, 2016).

(Isaiah 55:11). His faithfulness is one of the things that make Him God. He can always be depended upon. He is the same yesterday, today, and forever (Hebrews 13:8). "For I am the LORD, I do not change" (Malachi 3:6).

We can feel the intensity of Daniel's prayer. He was earnest. He was intense. He was sincere. Daniel's intercessory prayer that got God's attention. In fact, while Daniel was still praying, the LORD sent Gabriel with a message—the famous message about the seventy sevens, which is the foundation stone of biblical prophecy. Verse 20 says: "While I was speaking and praying, confessing my sin and the sin of my people Israel and making my request to the Lord my God for His holy hill—while I was still in prayer. . . (The LORD answered)."

So this chapter and indeed in this book, I would like to emphasize the power of intercessory prayers as a clear manifestation of holy lifestyle. Our nations in the world have been head-over-heels in chronic disobedience. In our own lives, we can experience areas of chronic disobedience. But Jesus came and died on the cross to forgive our disobedience and give us restoration. The secret is to do as Daniel did. As we pour into the Scriptures and as we study the Bible, it leads us to confession which can lead to intercession. Through Scriptures, we see how far we have fallen, or we see something we have failed to do, or we see something we have done that we need to confess. And as we confess, the LORD hears, and He answers, and He restores us to Himself and restores our fortunes. Intercessory prayers which include personal and national confession, manifest, the practicality of holiness in the life of believers. Holiness is none other than intercession for both personal and other people's affairs.

7

EZRA: A PURITAN REFORMER
AND YAHWEH'S PATRIOT

INTRODUCTION

EZRA (ACTIVE 5TH CENTURY B.C.) was a Hebrew priest, scribe, religious leader, and reformer who vitally reformed, influenced and reinforced Judaism. The son of Seraiah, Ezra was a descendant of the ancient priestly house of Zadok. . . Ezra is a biblical name meaning "help" or "helper" in Hebrew. Ezra helped reintroduce the Torah to the Israelites after they returned from captivity in Babylon. Soon after his arrival in Jerusalem, Ezra proceeded to reorganize the Temple and worship services. The second part of Ezra (7–10) begins with Ezra arriving in Jerusalem to teach God's laws to the people of Judah. . . So Ezra prayed and confessed Israel's sins, and the people agreed to begin obeying God's laws. Nehemiah's book reports other things that Ezra did.

Ezra's work helped reform Judaism **a religion in which law was central, enabling the Jews to survive as a community when they were dispersed all over the world. Since his efforts did much to give Jewish religion the form that was to charac**terize it for centuries later. With some justice Ezra has been called the father of Judaism; *i.e.,* the specific form the Jewish religion took after the Babylonian exile. So important was Ezra that later tradition regarded him as no less than a second Moses. Ezra was a priest and "a scribe skilled in the law." He represented the position of stricter Babylonian Jews who had been upset by reports of laxity in Judah and desired to see matters corrected. Ezra apparently had official status as a commissioner of the Persian government, and his title, "scribe of the law of the God of heaven," is best understood as "royal secretary for Jewish religious affairs," or the like. The delegated authority over the Jews of the satrapy (administrative area) "beyond the river" or west of the Euphrates River, was entrusted to Ezra. So for a Jew to disobey the Law he brought was to disobey "the law of the king."

It is said that Ezra came to Jerusalem **in the seventh year of King Artaxerxes (which Artaxerxes is not stated) of the Persian** dynasty **then ruling the area. Since he is introduced** before Nehemiah, who was governor of the province of Judah from 445 to 433 BC and again, after an interval, for a second term of unknown length, it is sometimes supposed that this was the seventh year of Artaxerxes I **(458 BC), though serious difficulties are attached to such a view.**[1] When Ezra arrived the situation in Judah was discouraging. Religious laxity was prevalent, the Law was widely disregarded, and public and private morality **was at a low level. Moreover, intermarriage with foreigners posed the threat that the community would mingle with the pagan** environment **and lose its identity.** The order in which Ezra took the various measures attributed to him is uncertain. He probably presented the Law to the people during the Feast of Tabernacles **in the autumn, most likely in the year of his arrival. He also took action against mixed marriages and succeeded in persuading**

---

1. Many scholars now believe that the biblical account is not chronological and that Ezra arrived in the 7th year of Artaxerxes II (397 BC), after Nehemiah had passed from the scene. Still others, holding that the two men were contemporaries, regard the 7th year as a scribal error and believe that perhaps Ezra arrived during Nehemiah's second term as governor. However, we leave this matter open. See https://bible.org/article/book-ezra (accessed on 18th May, 2021).

the people to divorce their foreign wives voluntarily. **His efforts reached their climax when the people engaged in solemn** cov- enant **before God to enter into no more mixed marriages, to refrain from work on the** Sabbath, to levy on themselves an an- nual tax for the support of the Temple, regularly to present their tithes and offerings, and otherwise to comply with the demands of the Law. The main theme of the Book is Ezra is the redemption of Israel and its reconstruction. Therefore, the book demonstrates God's role in this redemption.

EZRA AND NEHEMIAH: CONTEMPORARIES?

There have been three primary views with regard to the date of Ezra's return to Jerusalem. It is clear that the text joins his coming to Jerusalem with the reign of Artaxerxes, but which Artaxerxes is in view? If Artaxerxes I, Ezra returned in 458 BCE, the sev- enth year of the king's reign (Ezra 7:8). After completing certain reforms, it is conceivable that Ezra returned to Susa. Some thir- teen years later in 445, Nehemiah came to Jerusalem and began rebuilding the walls. He stayed for twelve years. During this twelve years Ezra returned again, and the two worked together reforming the exiles. This means that both Ezra and Nehemiah were for a time contemporaries, as is suggested by Nehemiah 8:2. This is the traditional view, but it is not without its problems. Why is Nehe- miah the governor not mentioned in Ezra? Further, why is Ezra only mentioned once in Nehemiah's memoirs and nothing is said of his reforms earlier in 458 BCE?

For these and other reasons, some scholars have developed other scenarios. It has been suggested that Ezra did not return under Artaxerxes I, but Artaxerxes II, in 398 BCE. This places Ezra after the time of Nehemiah. This seems to cohere better with the problem of marriage to foreign wives. If, under the traditional view, Ezra had dealt with that problem, why was it still an issue when Nehemiah arrived some thirteen or so years later? To some scholars it seems that Ezra came after Nehemiah, in the reign of Artaxerxes II, in 398. But that is not the only problem.[2]

THEOLOGICAL THEMES

The book of Ezra, in conjunction with Nehemiah, records the fulfillment of God's promise to restore his people to their land after seventy years of Babylonian captivity. In keeping with this, there is stress laid on God's sovereignty over both his own people, but also foreign kings and peoples as well. It was he who "stirred up the spirit" of Cyrus II (1:1) to permit any willing Israelite to return to his land. And it was he who later prompted Darius I (6:14, 22) and Artaxerxes I (7:11–13ff) to decree similarly (9:9).

Ezra also lays stress on the theme of God's covenant with his people, reflected especially in the Lord's special presence in the temple and Israel's special access to him through God-appointed sacrifice. Thus the rebuilding of the altar and the temple (Ezra 3–6), and the offering of sacrifices, receives considerable attention in Ezra. However, religious reform is essentially meaningless in Israelite theology without spiritual and ethical reform. Marriages to foreign women, though forbidden in the Law of Moses (cf. Ezra 9:11–12), were rampant during Ezra's time and posed an enormous threat to Israel's future commitment to remain true to YHWH. The solution was drastic, yet necessary: after Ezra's lengthy confession to God and plea for his mercy (9:5–15), the people decide to put their foreign wives away (10:19). Thus, the religious purity of the people was restored, if ever so briefly, through the work of Ezra. The overall focus in Ezra, then, is on the return of the LORD's people to

1. The worship of the God who keeps his covenant;

2. The land He promised to give his people;

3. Religious and ethical purity.

---

2. See https://bible.org/article/book-ezra (accessed on 18th May, 2021).

The books of Ezra and Nehemiah are about God's renewing His errant people. They are put together as one book in the Hebrew Bible, although the fact that the lists in Ezra 2 and Nehemiah 7 are virtually the same argues that originally they were separate. Ezra is about the return of the exiles from Babylon, the rebuilding of the Temple, and the restoration of God's people spiritually. Nehemiah is about the rebuilding of the walls of Jerusalem, as well as the spiritual renewal of God's people.

EZRA, THE INTERCESSORY REFORMER

Ezra, the priest, and one of Israel's great socio-religious and theological reformers, is shown as a praying man, one who uses prayer to overcome difficulties. He had returned from Babylon under the auspices of a foreign king, who had been strangely moved toward Ezra and favored him in many ways. Ezra had been in Jerusalem for a few days when the princes came to him with the distressing information that the people had not separated themselves from the people of that country, and were doing according to the abominations of the heathen nations about them. And that which was worse than all was that the princes and rulers in Israel had been chief in the trespass.

It was a sad state of affairs facing Ezra as he found the returning community of Israelites almost hopelessly involved with the world. God demands of His people in all ages that they should be separated from the world, a separation so sharp that it amounts to an antagonism. To effect this very end, He put Israel in the Promised Land, and cut them off from other nations by mountains, deserts and seas, and straightaway charged them that they should not form any relation with alien nations, neither in marital, social nor business. However, upon his return from exile, Ezra finds the Israelite community in Jerusalem and the whole Judea region paralyzed and hopelessly and thoroughly prostrated by the violation of their divine ordinances and precepts. They had intermarried, and had formed the closest and most sacred ties in family, social and business life, with the Gentile nations. Everyone was involved in it, priests, Levites, princes and people. What was to be done? What could be done? These were the important questions which faced Ezra in Israel. Everything appeared to be against the recovery of the community. Ezra could not preach to them, because the whole city would be inflamed, and would chase him out of the place. What force was there which could recover them to God so that they would dissolve business partnerships, divorce wives and husbands, cut acquaintances and dissolve friendships?

The first thing about Ezra which is worthy of remark was that he saw the situation and realized how serious it was. Ezra did not minimize the condition of things or seek to palliate the sins of the people or to minimize the enormity of their crimes. Their offense appeared in his eyes to be serious in the extreme. It is worth not a little to have leaders in Zion who have eyes to see the sins of the community of returnees as well as the evils of the times. He was distressed seeing these dreadful evils among the returnees and in the society of Jerusalem. The sad condition of things grieved him, so much so that he rent his garments, plucked his hair, and sat down astonished. All these things are evidences of his great distress of soul at the terrible state of affairs. Then it was in that frame of mind, concerned, solicitous and troubled in soul, that he gave himself to prayer, to confession of the sins of the people, and to pleading for pardoning mercy at the hands of God. To whom should he go in a time like this but unto the God who hears prayer, who is ready to pardon and who can bring the unexpected thing to pass? So, Ezra was amazed beyond expression at the wicked conduct of the people, was deeply moved and began to fast and pray. Prayer and fasting always accomplish something. He prays with a broken heart, for there is naught else that he can do. He prays unto God, deeply burdened, prostrate on the ground and weeping, while the whole city unites with him in prayer. For Ezra, prayer was the only way to placate God, and he became a great mover in a great work for God, with marvelous results. The whole work, its principles and its results, are summarized by just one verse in Ezra 10:1:

> Now when Ezra had prayed, and had confessed, weeping
> and casting himself down before the house of God, there

> assembled unto him out of Israel a very great congrega-
> tion of men and women and children, for the people
> wept sore.

Ezra's praying had brought forth results in a great work for God. It was mighty praying because it brought Almighty God to do His own work, which was absolutely hopeless from any other source save by prayer and by God. But nothing is hopeless to prayer because nothing is hopeless before God. Apparently, it must be stated that prayer has only to do with God, and is only resultful as it has to do with God. Whatever influence the praying of Ezra had upon himself, its chief result followed because it was to God, and it moved Him to do the work.

Therefore, a great and general repentance followed Ezra's prayer, and there occurred a wonderful revival and reformation in Israel. And Ezra's mourning and his praying were the great factors which had to do with bringing these great things to pass. So thorough was the revival which occurred that as evidences of its genuineness it is noted that the leaders in Israel came to Ezra with these words:

> We have trespassed against our God, and have taken
> strange wives of the people of the land. Yet now there is
> hope in Israel concerning this thing. Now therefore let us
> make a covenant with our God to put away all the wives,
> and such as are born to them, according to the counsel of
> my lord, and of those that tremble at the commandment
> of our God; and let it be done according to the law. Arise,
> for this matter belongs to you. We also will be with you;
> be of good courage, and do it.

The people acknowledged their sins and sought repentance. Where there are intercessory prayers, God intervene by coming down to revival his people. Ezra's prayers kindled God's gracious offer of renewal on his people in Israel.

ANALYSIS OF EZRA'S INTERCESSORY
PRAYER (EZRA 9:6–19A; 10:1–17)

Ezra's prayer, as a confession of national sin, should be compared with the prayer of the Levites (Nehemiah 9:6–38), and more especially with the prayer of Daniel (Daniel 9:4–19). As in the intercession of Daniel (personal and national confessions), the personality of the speaker is merged in that of the nation. The sin of the race no less than its shame and its punishment is acknowledged in the 'we', 'our', and 'us'. The self-abnegation and love of Ezra as of Moses (Exodus 32:32), as of Solomon (1 Kings 8), and of Paul (Romans 9:3), accept the obligations of nationality as the source of guilt as well as on privilege to the individual. In Ezra, the general plan of the intercession resembles that of Daniel. It consists of

1. General confession, Ezra 9:6 (*cf.* Daniel 9:4–6),

2. The sins of former time, Ezra 9:7 (cf. Daniel 9:7–8);

3. God's mercy and goodness, Ezra 9:7–8 (cf. Daniel 9:9);

4. Israel's sin in the face of the Divine warning, Ezra 9:10–12 (cf. Daniel 9:10–14);

5. The fresh guilt and final appeal, Ezra 9:13–15 (cf. Daniel 9:15–19).

Therefore, as Ezra prayed, he alone prayed—yet because he stood before an assembly of the people of God, there was a sense in which he led them in prayer. Indeed, even in our own times, the pastor or minister is not merely to pray before the congregation, while the people kneel as silent auditors. His prayer is designed to guide and help their prayers, so that there may be 'common prayer' throughout the whole assembly.

Ezra did how it was done in most cases in the Old Testament, i.e., spreading out *his* hands to the LORD. In our contemporary times, many close their eyes, bow their head, and fold their hands as they pray, but the Old Testament tradition was to spread out the hands toward heaven in a gesture of surrender, openness, and ready reception. "With the palms open toward heaven, in a having, craving way, as beggars. This was the Jewish manner of praying, and it was very becoming": *O my God, I am ashamed and blush.* Indeed, nothing can be more humble, devout, and pathetic, than this address, in which Ezra acknowledges that he was confounded when he thought of the greatness of their sins, which were ready to overwhelm them, and of the boldness and insolence of them beyond measure, even though they had seen the divine vengeance upon their forefathers in so terrible a manner, that they had not yet worn off the marks of his displeasure. He had, indeed, begun to show favour to some of them; but this so much the more aggravated their wickedness, in that, so soon after their restoration and settlement in their native country, they had returned to their old provocations, notwithstanding the many admonitions, in the law and the prophets, to have nothing to do with the people of Canaan.

Ezra's address is a penitent intercession for the people's sins. But let this be the comfort of true penitents, that though their sins reach to the heavens, God's mercy is in the heavens. Ezra included himself in the number of the transgressors, because he himself was guilty of many sins; and because the princes and priests, and so many of the people, having done this, the guilt had become national. Yes, while Ezra was praying, and while he was confessing. While Ezra was praying, and while he was confessing, weeping, and bowing down before the house of God, a very large assembly of people gathered to him and they wept very bitterly. The power of Ezra's confession was not merely in the words recorded in Ezra 9:6–15. It was in the depth of heart that brought forth the prayer, here evidence by weeping, and bowing down before the house of God. He prayed this prayer and humbled himself on behalf of the people publicly.

"Bowing down before the house of God:" This implies that Ezra kept on 'throwing himself down' on the ground." Then Ezra arose, and made the leaders of the priests, the Levites, and all Israel swear an oath that they would do according to this word. So they swore an oath. Then Ezra rose up from before the house of God, and went into the chamber of Jehohanan the son of Eliashib; and when he came there, he ate no bread and drank no water, for he mourned because of the guilt of those from the captivity. And they issued a proclamation throughout Judah and Jerusalem to all the descendants of the captivity, that they must gather at Jerusalem, and that whoever would not come within three days, according to the instructions of the leaders and elders, all his property would be confiscated, and he himself would be separated from the assembly of those from the captivity.

So, all the men of Judah and Benjamin gathered at Jerusalem within three days. It was the ninth month, on the twentieth of the month; and all the people sat in the open square of the house of God, trembling because of this matter and because of heavy rain. Then Ezra the priest stood up and said to them, "You have transgressed and have taken pagan wives, adding to the guilt of Israel. Now therefore, make confession to the LORD God of your fathers, and do His will; separate yourselves from the peoples of the land, and from the pagan wives." Then all the assembly answered and said with a loud voice, "Yes! As you have said, so we must do. But there are many people; it is the season for heavy rain, and we are not able to stand outside. Nor is this the work of one or two days, for there are many of us who have transgressed in this matter. Please, let the leaders of our entire assembly stand; and let all those in our cities who have taken pagan wives come at appointed times, together with the elders and judges of their cities, until the fierce wrath of our God is turned away from us in this matter." Only Jonathan the son of Asahel and Jahaziah the son of Tikvah opposed this, and Meshullam and Shabbethai the Levite gave them support.

Relating intercession to holiness, which is a setting apart from one's sinful practices, Ezra was truly a holy reformer who zealously acted in accordance to the divine mandate of holiness as separation. Ezra's holy lifestyle threw him to intercede for the people of Israel. It thrusted him to lead them into confession of their sins as individuals and as a nation. Indeed, holiness should always be exemplified in one's hating of what is evil and sinful and to pray for those indulging themselves in such.

LESSONS FROM EZRA'S INTERCESSORY PRAYERS

1. Intercessory prayer goes hand in hand with confession;

2. The godly reaction to sin is to mourn over it;

3. The godly reaction to sin is to confess it without excuse to the God of mercy;

4. Confession acknowledges the absolute righteousness of God in all his dealings with us;

5. Confession submits to God's righteous dealings without complaint or excuse;

6. Confession agrees with God concerning his view of our sin;

7. Confession casts the sinner on God's undeserved mercy, based on the sacrifice of Jesus Christ;

8. Dealing with sin starts with the right heart attitude;

9. Dealing with sin needs strategic and operational plans;

10. Dealing with sin can at times be messy;

11. Dealing with sin is most successful when there is accountability;

12. Dealing with sin at times takes radical measures;

13. Dealing with sin requires a right attitude about the serious nature of holiness;

14. Intercessory prayer is both personal and communal.

C. S. Lewis observed, "When a man is getting better, he understands more and more clearly the evil that is still in him. When a man is getting worse, he understands his own badness less and less."[3] As we grow in godliness and holiness, with Ezra we will react more strongly to our own sins and to the sins of other people. We will dwell more consistently at the foot of the cross of Jesus Christ, where God's mercy flows to repentant sinners.[4]

3. Cited by Nathan Hatch, *Christianity Today* [3/2/79], p. 14.

4. https://bible.org/seriespage/lesson-9-godly-reaction-sin-ezra-91–15 (accessed on 18th May, 2021).

CONCLUSION

This chapter has discussed Ezra's intercessory role in ancient Israel. We have observed his attitude and posture for God's forgiveness of human sins. Ezra's intercessory prayers portrays how to deal with sin of any kind. What is our attitude toward sin? Do we react like Ezra did? Do we really hate sin like God because He is holy? Or do we tolerate it like the world around us? When is the last time our sin caused us a certain level of sadness? The story of Ezra teaches us many important lessons. One lesson is that our sins can lead us into situations from which there is no good way out. Therefore, the only way out of such is to take some radical measures. The best solution is confession for both us as individuals and for others as corporate community that we are entangled with. This is a positive attitude toward God's demand of holiness on our part. In this chapter I have demonstrated that Ezra prayed:

> "O LORD God of Israel, You *are* righteous, for we are left as a remnant, as *it is* this day. Here we *are* before You, in our guilt, though no one can stand before You because of this!"

Here, Ezra wisely appealed to the LORD as the God of Israel. Although they had been unfaithful to Him, Ezra still hoped for covenant mercies from the LORD because He was their God. Ezra also wisely appealed to God's righteousness, especially in leaving a remnant in fulfillment of His prior promises.[5]

Therefore, "Ezra is far too much in earnest simply to wish to help his people to escape from the consequences of their conduct. This would not be salvation. It would be moral shipwreck. The great need is to be saved from the evil conduct itself." Ezra wisely did not claim an excuse or a reason for their sin. Israel had sinned and they were guilty. The appeal must be made for mercy to the guilty, not as a favor to the deserving (or semi-deserving). It must be noted here that Ezra also did not claim special circumstances or did he tell God that their difficult environment made their present

---

5. See 2 Chronicles 30:6; Isaiah 10:20–22.

compromise understandable, or that all their other good works or faithfulness somehow excused their idolatry. He simply realized that no one can stand before You because of this! "Ezra had not even the heart to plead, as Moses had, that God's name would suffer in such a case. His prayer was naked intercessory prayers that focused on confession, without excuses, without the pressure of so much as a request.

8

JESUS: YAHWEH'S BELOVED SON[1]

INTRODUCTION: JESUS, THE SON OF GOD

JESUS, ALSO CALLED JESUS CHRIST, JESUS of Galilee, or Jesus of Nazareth, (born c. 6–4 BCE, Bethlehem—died c. 30 CE, Jerusalem), a religious leader revered in Christianity, one of the world's major religions. He is regarded by most Christians as the incarnation of God. Ancient Jews usually had only one name, and, when greater specificity was needed, it was customary to add the father's name or the place of origin. Thus, in his lifetime Jesus was called Jesus son of Joseph (Luke 4:22; John 1:45, 6:42), Jesus of Nazareth (Acts 10:38), or Jesus the Nazarene (Mark 1:24; Luke 24:19).

After his death he came to be called Jesus Christ. *Christ* was not originally a name but a title derived from the Greek word *christos*, which translates the Hebrew term *meshiah* (Messiah), meaning "the anointed one." This title indicates that Jesus' followers believed him to be the anointed son of King David, whom some Jews expected to restore the kingdom of Israel. Passages such as Acts of the Apostles 2:36 show that some early Christian writers knew that *the Christ* was properly a title, but in many passages of

1. See John 3:16, Galatians 4:4, among others.

the New Testament, including those in the letters of the Apostle Paul, the name and title are combined and used together as Jesus' name: Jesus Christ or Christ Jesus (Romans 1:1; 3:24). Paul sometimes simply used Christ as Jesus' name (e.g., Romans 5:6).

In the Gospel of John, the Bible calls Jesus "the Son of God" (John 1:49). The expression "Son of God" acknowledges that God is the Creator, or Source, of all life, including that of Jesus (Psalm 36:9; Revelation 4:11). The Bible does not teach that God literally fathered a child in the same way that humans produce children. In the fullness of time, God sent his only Son to redeem his good but defaced creation (Galatians 4:4). God's Son, is the epitome of the Story of Salvation as described in the pages of the Bible from the first book of the Bible—Genesis to the last book of the Bible—Revelation. Jesus is God's Son in the sense that He is God made manifest in human form (John 1:1, 14). Jesus is God's Son in that He was conceived in Mary by the Holy Spirit. Luke 1:35 declares, "The angel answered, 'The Holy Spirit will come upon you, and the power of the Most High will overshadow you. So, the holy one to be born will be called the Son of God.'"

During His trial before the Jewish leaders, the High Priest demanded of Jesus, "I charge you under oath by the living God: Tell us if you are the Christ, the Son of God" (Matthew 26:63). "'Yes, it is as you say,' Jesus replied. 'But I say to all of you: In the future you will see the Son of Man sitting at the right hand of the Mighty One and coming on the clouds of heaven'" (Matthew 26:64). The Jewish leaders responded by accusing Jesus of blasphemy (Matthew 26:65–66). Later, before Pontius Pilate, "The Jews insisted, 'We have a law, and according to that law He must die, because He claimed to be the Son of God'" (John 19:7). Why would His claiming to be the Son of God be considered blasphemy and be worthy of a death sentence? The Jewish leaders understood exactly what Jesus meant by the phrase "Son of God." To be the Son of God is to be of the same nature as God. The Son of God is "of God." The claim to be of the same nature as God—to in fact be God—was blasphemy to the Jewish leaders; therefore, they demanded Jesus' death, in keeping with Leviticus 24:15. Hebrews 1:3 expresses this very clearly, "The Son is the radiance of God's glory and the exact representation of His being.²"

JESUS'S MINISTRY

The Bible tells us that Jesus is our great Intercessor. An intercessor is one who prays for another. And that is just what the Lord Jesus is doing now. He is in Heaven praying for all those who believe on Him. There were many great men in the Bible who prayed for others. They interceded with God for their people. We have discussed a lot of biblical personalities and their character and how they lived their life style of holiness which was exemplified in interceding for others. Intercession is an ongoing work of Christ our high priest. His sin offering is a finished work which never needs repeating. Not all Christ's work is finished, however, because he now continues to make intercession for us in heaven. This is where we talk of the "complete" atonement accomplished by Jesus Christ on the cross, and the "completed" atonement in relationship to His intercessory ministry in heaven on humanity's behalf. Nothing can improve or supplement Jesus' salvific work, and no one can add anything to Christ's sacrificial officering of himself for humanity; salvation is "complete" (Rom 3:21–26; 1 Cor 1:18, 23–24; 2:2; Gal 2:16, 21; Ephesians 2:4–10). Jesus' mediatory work was made possible only because of this exceptional, unselfish, and once-for-all death for humanity (Hebrews 9:28). The Bible powerfully declares that Jesus Christ is presently in heaven (Mark 16:19; Luke 24:50–51; Acts 1:9–11) and is interceding for humans (hinted to in Rom 5:10–21, but explicitly taught in Rom 8:34; 1 John 2:1). This fundamental teaching attests that Christ's intermediatory role is urgently needed to accomplish the plan of salvation. Jesus Christ is our Intercessor and serves as our Mediator, our High Priest, in the heavenly sanctuary (Hebrews 4:15–16; 8:1–2).³ As Christians,

2. For more information on this, see the Church history books, which debate ancient issues on Christology and other theological issues.

3. Three times Jesus Christ is called the Mediator in the book of Hebrews and always in relation to a new or better covenant (8:6; 9:15; 12:24).

not only can we step in the gap and intercede and pray for someone else for whatever their prayer need may be, but we can also ask both Jesus and the Holy Spirit to step into the gap and pray for us and with us to God the Father on that specific prayer request.

This chapter discusses the ministry of Jesus in fulfilling what was written by the Prophets and the Psalms in the Old Testament. However, emphasis will be laid upon his intercessory ministry.

> As the soldiers led him away, they seized Simon from Cyrene, who was on his way in from the country, and put the cross on him and made him carry it behind Jesus. [27]A large number of people followed him, including women who mourned and wailed for him. [28]Jesus turned and said to them, "Daughters of Jerusalem, do not weep for me; weep for yourselves and for your children. [29]For the time will come when you will say, 'Blessed are the childless women, the wombs that never bore and the breasts that never nursed!' [30] Then "'they will say to the mountains, "Fall on us!" and to the hills, "Cover us!"' [31] For if people do these things when the tree is green, what will happen when it is dry?" Now there were some present at that time who told Jesus about the Galileans whose blood Pilate had mixed with their sacrifices. Jesus answered, "Do you think that these Galileans were worse sinners than all the other Galileans because they suffered this way? I tell you, no! But unless you repent, you too will all perish. Or those eighteen who died when the tower in Siloam fell on them—do you think they were more guilty than all the others living in Jerusalem? I tell you, no! But unless you repent, you too will all perish."

JESUS' SORROW FOR JERUSALEM

[31]At that time some Pharisees came to Jesus and said to him, "Leave this place and go somewhere else. Herod wants to kill you." [32] He replied, "Go tell that fox, 'I will keep on driving out demons and healing people today and tomorrow, and on the third day I will reach

my goal.' [33] In any case, I must press on today and to-morrow and the next day—for surely no prophet can die outside Jerusalem! [34] "Jerusalem, Jerusalem, you who kill the prophets and stone those sent to you, how often I have longed to gather your children together, as a hen gathers her chicks under her wings, and you were not willing. [35] Look, your house is left to you desolate. I tell you, you will not see me again until you say, 'Blessed is he who comes in the name of the Lord.'"

ANALYSIS OF JESUS INTERCESSORY MINISTRY

Jesus Christ's role as Intercessor could be identified to be twofold in nature:[4]

1. Revealing and ministering the mysteries of God's goodness and richness to humankind;

2. Presenting our existential needs to God and securing our salvation.

Jesus' intercessory ministry is both a revelatory and redemptive process for humanity, forming one unit that cannot be separated. Alister McGrath correctly explains that

> The presence of God in Christ is intended to mediate between a transcendent God and fallen humanity. This idea of 'presence as mediation' takes two quite distinct, yet ultimately complementary, forms: the mediation of revelation on the one hand, and of salvation on the other.[5]

4. See Jesus' intercessory ministry—Search (bing.com) (accessed on 20 July 2022). See also Jiri Moskala, "The Meaning of the Intercessory Ministry of Jesus Christ on Our Behalf in the Heavenly Sanctuary" "The Intercessory Ministry of Jesus Christ in the Heavenly Sanctuary" by Jiri Moskala ThD, PhD (andrews.edu)

5. Alister E. McGrath, *Christian Theology: An Introduction* (Cambridge, Mass.: Blackwell Publishers, 1997), 346, 347.

Jesus Christ is able to be our go-between, i.e., mediator who can speak to God on our behalf. We can then "draw near to God through him" (Hebrews 7:25). The prophecy about Christ stated that "he himself bore the sin of many and interceded for the transgressors" (Isaiah 53:12). Therefore, it stands to reason that someone who is in much the same position as ourselves, someone who needs an intercessor as much as we do, is not qualified in his own right to intercede for us. Only Jesus and the Holy Spirit are qualified to be our intercessors.[6]

There is only one priest among men who cannot go to God in his own right and intercede for us, who himself does not need an intercessor. That man is Jesus Christ. That is one reason why he said, "I am the way, the truth and the life; no one can come to the father except through me" (John 14:6). We have an advocate, Jesus the Christ, it is He who is our defense. Jesus is our intercessor; this means He is the bridge that will ultimately connect us back to God the Father.

First of all, Jesus' divinity (John 1:1–3; Rom. 9:5; Col. 1:15–18) represents the Godhead. As the mediator of the divine, he reveals the Father, his character, and all the values of the Godhead (Matt. 11:27; Luke 10:22; John 1:14–18; 17:6), because he and the Father are one (John 10:30). Even the Old Testament paints the picture of God mediating for his people (1 Sam. 2:25; Job 16:20). Christ also discloses the Holy Spirit by explaining the Spirit's ministry (John 14:16, 17; 15:26, 27; 16:7–15), also of interceding for the saints (Rom. 8:27). With the entrance of sin (Gen. 3:1–10) and the ensuing distortion of God's character, Christ's birth and great sacrifice on the cross for humanity demonstrated credibly and convincingly that God is the God of love, truth, and justice (John 3:16; rom. 1:16, 17; 3:21–26; 5:5–8).

Second, Jesus Christ by experiencing true humanity (Matt. 4:1–11; Rom. 8:3; Col. 2:9; 1 John 1:1, 2; 4:2, 3) understands our struggles (Heb. 4:15, 16), and thus, as our representative (1 Tim. 2:5) he can efficiently mediate on our behalf between the Holy Father and sinful humanity. The scriptures certainly attest that Jesus

6. Romans 8:26, 34.

Christ intercedes on our behalf before the heavenly Father (Rom. 8:34; Heb. 7:25; 9:24) and that he is our advocate (1 John 2:1). The movement is clearly that of uplifting believers in God from earth to the heavenly Father.

Jesus is mediator, but. . .the title means more than someone between God and man. . . . As true God he brings God to mankind. As true man he brings mankind to God. Taking is from the Bible's revelation, most Christians generally consider Jesus to be the Christ, the long-awaited Messiah, as well as the one and only Son of God. Therefore, speaking of Jesus, the writer to the Hebrews says, "Therefore He is able also to save forever those who draw near to God through Him, since He always lives to make intercession for them" (Hebrews 7:25). This verse (and others like it) tells us that although Christ's work to secure the salvation of the elect was completed on the cross, as evidenced by His cry "It is finished!" (John 19:30), His care for His redeemed children will never be finished. This means that Jesus did not go to heaven after His earthly ministry and "take a break" from His role as eternal Shepherd to His people. "For if while we were enemies we were reconciled to God through the death of His Son, much more, having been reconciled, we shall be saved by His life" (Romans 5:10). If when humble, despised, dying, and dead, He had the power to accomplish so great a work as reconciling us to God, how much more may we expect that He will be able to keep us now that He is a living, exalted, and triumphant Redeemer, raised to life and interceding on our behalf before the throne (Romans 8:34). Clearly, Jesus is still very active interceding on our behalf in heaven.

After Jesus ascended to heaven and was seated at the right hand of God the Father (Acts 1:9; Colossians 3:1), He returned to the glory He had before His incarnation (John 17:5) to carry on His role of King of kings and Lord of lords—His eternal role as the Second Person of the triune God. While this old earth continues to be "won" for Christ, Jesus is the Advocate for Christians, i.e., He is our great Defender. This is the intercessory role He currently fulfills for those who are His (1 John 2:1). Jesus is always pleading our case before the Father, like a defense lawyer on our behalf.

Jesus is interceding for us while Satan (whose name means "accuser") is accusing us, pointing out our sins and frailties before God, just as he did with Job (Job 1:6–12). But the accusations fall upon deaf ears in heaven, because Jesus' work on the cross paid our sin debt in full. Therefore, God always sees in His children the perfect righteousness of Jesus. When Jesus died on the cross, His righteousness (perfect holiness) was imputed to us, while our sin was imputed to Him at His death. This is the great exchange Paul talks about in 2 Corinthians 5:21. That took away forever our sinful state before God, so God can accept us as blameless before Him. Of course, not only did Jesus's death imputed on us his righteousness, the same also imparted in us his righteousness and holiness.

Finally, it is important to understand that Jesus is the only human mediator between God and man. No one else—not Mary, Rastafari, not Krishna, not Shiva, no Buddha, not Confucius, not the Dalai Lama, not Zoroaster, not Muhammad, not any previous Christian saints—has the power to intercede for us before the throne of Yahweh, the Almighty God. No angel has that position and responsibility. Christ alone is the God-man, and He alone mediates and intercedes between God and man. "For there is one God, and one mediator also between God and men, the man Christ Jesus" (1 Timothy 2:5).

A few fundamental issues about Jesus as the intercessor for us in heaven abode are in order here:

1. "Who is he who condemns? It is Christ who died, and furthermore is also risen, who is even at the right hand of God, who also makes intercession for us" (Romans 8:34).

2. "Therefore He is also able to save to the uttermost those who come to God through Him, since He ever lives to make intercession for them" (Hebrews 7:25).

3. "Likewise the Spirit also helps in our weaknesses. For we do not know what we should pray for as we ought, but the Spirit Himself makes intercession for us *with groanings which cannot be uttered. Now He who searches the hearts knows what*

the mind of the Spirit is, because He makes intercession for the saints according to the will of God" (Romans 8:26–27).

CONCLUSION

Jesus Christ is able to be our go-between and He speaks to God on our behalf. We can then "draw near to God through him" (Hebrews 7:25). The prophecy about Christ stated that "He himself bore the sin of many and interceded for the transgressors" (Isaiah 53:12). There is only one priest among men who can go to God in his own right and intercede for us, who himself does not need an intercessor. That man is Jesus Christ.

As Christians, we are greatly blessed in having a great High Priest, one who ever lives to make intercession for us. John describes him as our "Advocate with the Father" (1 John 2:1–2). Jesus understands our weaknesses without himself being weak. There is no one closer to God than he. Through him we can come to God and find utmost grace. Hence, the encouragement, "Let us therefore come boldly to the throne of grace that we may receive mercy and find grace to help in time of need" (Hebrews 4:16). And again, "Let us draw near with a sincere heart in full assurance of faith. . ." (Hebrews 10:22).

Therefore, the willingness of Christians to evangelize and of sinners to repent does make the difference in the matter of who will spend eternity with God and who will suffer forever without Him. The unwillingness of men creates the tragedy of lost opportunity over which Jesus is weeping in the book of Luke. The following summarizes the four main functions of Jesus Christ as our Intercessor:

1. On Jesus Christ's return to heaven, He and the heavenly Father met together to help humans in their everyday struggles with evil. The first tangible result of that meeting on our behalf was that the Holy Spirit was given to believers (Acts 2). All heaven is united in helping us in our struggles with sin, Satan, and temptations (John 15:5; Phil. 4:13). Jesus prays

JESUS: YAHWEH'S BELOVED SON

for us (John 17; Luke 22:32), and our best—and worst—is covered by Christ's perfect life and atoning sacrifice. We are enabled through His power to witness to others.

2. Jesus Christ saves completely and identifies with us when we give our life to Him (Zech. 2:8; Matt. 25:40, 45; Acts 9:4–6). He saves, justifies, sanctifies, and changes believers into His image (Zech. 3:1–7). Because of His goodness (Rom. 2:4; Eph. 1:7), we identify with Him (Rom. 6:1–4; Eph. 2:4–10).

3. Jesus Christ's intercessory ministry transforms His followers into His likeness, they grow in Him and His grace, and become more and more like Him (2 Cor. 3:18; 2 Peter 1:3, 4; 3:18).

4. Jesus Christ vindicates us against the accusations of Satan (Rev. 12:10–12; Job 1:8, 9; 2:4; 42). He personally stands up against them; and because He is the Victor, our victory is secure in Him when we accept Him as the Lord of our life.

Therefore, knowing this magnificent work of Jesus Christ "for" and "in" us, one cannot do otherwise than give Him glory. Wesleyan scholarship speaks of these two terms: 'for' and 'in' representing Christ's work in the world. His death brings imputed righteousness for us. His death brings the imparted righteousness in us. The two terms and concepts must never be misinterpreted and misrepresented or emphasizing one over against the other.

9

PAUL: GOD'S BONDSERVANT AND APOSTLE PER EXCELLENCE[1]

INTRODUCTION

PAUL, ORIGINALLY CALLED SAUL, was a Jewish lawyer—trained under a great legal mind, Gamaliel in Jerusalem. Paul was both a Jewish man as well as a Roman citizen of the Cilicia, now Turkey, recently changed to Turkiye,[2] a province under the Roman Empire of the first century AD. Paul was one of the most influential leaders of the early Christian church. He played a very crucial role in spreading the gospel in the Mediterranean world. His missionary journeys took him all throughout the Roman Empire. Paul is traditionally considered to have written more than 13 epistles on the New Testament section of the Bible—apparently, more than any other writer of the Bible.

According to the New Testament book Acts of the Apostles (often called the Book of Acts or simply Acts), Paul participated in

1. See Acts 9:15–16 where Paul is also called the Instrument for carrying God's name—the message of God's salvation to all mankind. See also Colossians 1:23.

2. Recently in 2022, the name has been changed to Turkiye.

the persecution of early disciples of Jesus, possibly Hellenized diaspora Jews converted to Christianity, in the area of Jerusalem, prior to his conversion. In the narrative of Acts, Paul was traveling on the road from Jerusalem to Damascus on a mission to "arrest them and bring them back to Jerusalem" when the ascended Jesus appeared to him in a great bright light. He was struck blind, but after three days his sight was restored by Ananias of Damascus and Paul began to preach that Jesus of Nazareth was the Jewish messiah and the Son of God. Approximately half of the Book of Acts deals with Paul's life and works. The two main sources of information that give access to the earliest segments of Paul's career are the Book of Acts and the autobiographical elements of Paul's letters to the early Christian communities.[3] Paul was likely born between the years of 5 BC and 5 AD.[4] The Book of Acts indicates that Paul was a Roman citizen by birth.

Before Paul became a disciple and missionary of Christianity, he was a prime example of a righteous Jew. He came from a God-fearing family—2 Timothy 1:3; he was a Pharisee like his father—Acts 23:6; and he was educated by a respected Jewish legal rabbi name Gamaliel—Acts 22:3. Paul's Jewish credentials therefore included his heritage, discipline and his zeal. In Philippians 3, he explains why if anyone ever had reasons to believe that they could be saved by their adherence to Judaism, it was him:

> If someone else thinks they have reasons to put confidence in the flesh, I have more: circumcised on the eighth day, of the people of Israel, of the tribe of Benjamin, a Hebrew of Hebrews; in regard to the law a Pharisee; as for zeal, persecuting the church; as for righteousness based on the law, faultless.[5]

Paul's identity used to be rooted in his Jewishness. However, after his conversion on the road to Damascus, his identity as a Jew

3. Dunn, James D. G., ed. (2003), *The Cambridge Companion to St. Paul*, Cambridge: Cambridge University Press, ISBN 0-521-78155-8

4. White, L. Michael (2007). *From Jesus to Christianity*. San Francisco, CA: Harper Collins. ISBN 978-0-06-081610-0.

5. Philippians 3: 4-6.

became secondary to his identity as a follower of Jesus Christ—whom he has been crucified with.

PAUL'S PATTERN AND HABITS OF PRAYER

These are revealed almost unconsciously. He writes (Rom. 1. 9), "God is my witness that without ceasing I make mention of you always in my prayers. For I long to see you, that I may impart unto you some spiritual gift, to the end ye may be established." Romana 10:1; 9: 2, 3: "My heart's desire and prayer to God for Israel is, that they may be saved;" "I have great heaviness and continual sorrow of heart; for I could wish that myself were accursed from Christ for my brethren." 1 Cor. 1:4: "I thank my God always on your behalf, for the grace of God which is given you by Jesus Christ." 2 Cor. 6: 4, 6: "Approving ourselves as the ministers of Christ, in watchings, in fastings." Gal. 4: 19: "My little children, of whom travail in birth again till Christ be formed in you." Eph. 1: 16: "I cease not to give thanks for you, making mention of you in my prayers." Eph. 3: 14: "I bow my knees to the Father, that He would grant you to be strengthened with might by His Spirit in the inner man." Phil. 1: 3, 4, 8, 9: "I thank my God upon every remembrance of you, always in every prayer of mine making request for you all with joy. For God is my record, how greatly I long after you all in the bowels of Jesus Christ. And this I pray"— Col. 1: 3, 9: "We give thanks to God, praying always for you. For this cause also, since the day we heard it, we do not cease to pray for you, and to desire"— Col. 2: 1: "I would that ye knew what great conflict I have for you, and for as many as have not seen my face in the flesh." 1 Thess. 3:9: "We joy for your sakes before God; night and day praying exceedingly that we might perfect that which is lacking in your faith." 2 Thess. 1: 3: "We are bound to thank God always for you. Wherefore also we always pray for you." 2 Tim. 1: 3: "I thank God, that without ceasing I have remembrance of thee night and day." Philem. 1: 4: "I thank my God, making mention of thee always in my prayers." "I always thank my God as I remember you in my prayers, because I hear about your faith in the Lord Jesus and your love for all the saints. I pray that you may be active in sharing your faith, so that you will have a full understanding of every good thing we have in Christ. Your love has given me great joy and encouragement, because you, brother, have refreshed the hearts of the saints" (Philemon 4–7).

These passages taken together give us the picture of a man whose words, "Pray without ceasing," were simply the expression of his daily life. He had such a sense of the insufficiency of simple conversion; of the need of the grace and the power of heaven being brought down for the young converts in prayer; of the need of much and unceasing prayer, day and. night, to bring it down; of the certainty that prayer would bring it down; that his life was continual and most definite prayer. He had such a sense that everything must come from above, and such a faith that it would come in answer to prayer, that prayer was neither a duty nor a burden, but the natural turning of the heart to the only place whence it could possibly obtain what it sought for others.

ANALYSIS OF THE APOSTLE PAUL'S INTERCESSORY MINISTRY

In Romans chapters 9–11 Paul is dealing with a couple of subjects; one the sovereignty of God, but it is the sovereignty of God in setting aside the nation Israel as God's primary target, you might say for work, and beginning to pour out His Spirit and work among the Gentiles. Because Paul is a Jew through and through, his heart, his prayer for Israel is that they might be saved, and yet, he can see in the Scriptures those prophecies of God's move among the Gentiles. In the later portion of chapter 10, he gives some of those prophecies of how God was going to be found of them that did not seek for Him; He was going to manifest Himself unto the Gentiles, but of the Jew He said, "All day long have I stretched out my hands unto a disobedient and gainsaying people."

> Brothers and sisters, my heart's desire and prayer to God for the Israelites is that they may be saved. For I

can testify about them that they are zealous for God, but their zeal is not based on knowledge. Since they did not know the righteousness of God and sought to establish their own, they did not submit to God's righteousness.[6] I ask then: Did God reject his people? By no means! I am an Israelite myself, a descendant of Abraham, from the tribe of Benjamin. God did not reject his people, whom he foreknew.[7]

The apostle Paul was not a Jew-hater. He himself was a Jew, and he expressed his love for his fellow Jews in this unique manner: *". . . I have great sorrow and continual grief in my heart. For I could wish that I myself were accursed from Christ for my brethren, my countrymen according to the flesh"* (Romans 9:2,3). Yes, Paul was *"an apostle to the Gentiles"* (Romans 11:13), but he preached with intenseness to the Jews, too.

So what was it that Paul wanted to happen in the lives of his fellow Jews? *"Brethren, my heart's desire and prayer to God for Israel is that they may be saved"* (Romans 10:1). There you have it: Paul wanted the Jews to be saved. Many were. The majority, however, were not, and that troubled Paul, causing him sorrow and grief (9:2).

Paul was not silent about his heart's longing for Israel's salvation. He communicated that desire to the saints in Rome (10:1), he expressed that desire in prayer to God (10:1), and he told the Jews face to face that he preached Jesus to them so they could receive the forgiveness of sins through Him (Acts 13:37–39). What about you and me? Do we express to lost people that we care about their souls? Paul prayed for the Jews to be converted. Do you and I pray for those whom we love to be saved? The time to offer such prayers is now, while both they and we are still alive. Once that loved one or friend has left this world, there is no benefit in praying for them. After their exodus, our actions or words on earth have no bearing whatsoever on their spiritual condition. In fact, it is disturbing to think that a Christian would ask God to have

6. Romans 10:1–3.

7. Romans 11:11.

mercy on and forgive a dead person of his/her sins, knowing that that person never obeyed the gospel on earth. While a person is still alive – *that* is the time to pray for them. While a person is still living on earth – *that* is the time for them to submit to the Lord and obtain His mercy.

Paul's desire for the Jews' salvation was limited in its power and influence. What does that mean? Simply this: Paul could not override or negate the desire of the Jews themselves. The apostle's will was for all Jews to become followers of Jesus. However, that would and could happen only if *they* wanted to do it. Paul longed for the Jews' salvation and he prayed about it, but he could not force the Jews to receive the gospel. God wants all people to be saved, too (1 Timothy 2:4), but His desire does not remove a person's freedom of choice.

What else could Paul do to help bring about the salvation of the Jews? He could put his desire into action, which is exactly what he did. Paul did more than pray and talk about the Jews being saved—he gave his best effort to teach them the good news of Jesus' salvation. Any person, Jew or non-Jew, can be saved only through Jesus (Acts 4:12). Paul knew that the gospel is God's power to salvation (Romans 1:16), so he taught the Jews what they needed to hear, the only message that could educate them properly and save their soul. Check him out. There he is preaching to Jews in crowded synagogues (Acts 17:1-3). There he is reaching out to a group of Jewish women at the riverside in Philippi (Acts 16:13-15). There he is talking with anyone who would listen in the marketplace in Athens (Acts 17:17). There he is standing on the stairs and speaking openly to Jews in Jerusalem about Jesus of Nazareth (Acts 21:40- 22:21). You get the picture.

Therefore, in the epistle to the Romans, Paul emphatically says that he wished he himself were accursed for the sake of his own race—the Hebrews, Jewish people. His prayer was the God continues to remember these descendants of his friend—Abraham. This can be noticed from the fact that, although he was an apostle appointed specifically to the gentile world, his ministry was, in most cases, first and foremost to the Jews who would reject him and his message, then afterwards he could indeed turn to the gentiles. So the question is, has God cast away His people? Is He through with them forever? God forbid. The whole prophecy picture of the Old Testament dealt with Israel's fall, but in order that they might rise again.

He says, "My heart's desire and my prayer to God for them." There is a lot to say about this. He has a heart desire. Paul is not a cold, lukewarm, stoic, hyper-intellect who has no emotions. Paul is a brilliant intellect and he is an astute theologian, but it is in no way divorced from having a heart of passionate zeal for those who are without Christ. Paul has a felt religion, and you and I need to have a felt religion, an affectionate religion. You and I need to know what it is to have our heart filled with great affection for God, affection for believers, affection for those who are without Christ. And that is what Paul is expressing here.

And this is just really the tip of the iceberg for all this within the depths of Paul's heart. And that desire is expressed in prayer. He says, "My heart's desire and my prayer to God for them." It wasn't enough that Paul just felt something for those without Christ; he must do something for those who are without Christ. And the greatest thing that you can do for someone without Christ is to pray for their salvation and to witness to them. Paul is unable to witness to the entire nation of Israel but he can certainly pray for them. And that is what Paul is expressing that he does. The word intercession for "prayer" is an important word for prayer, and it is a rather aggressive word. And it means to be pleading and petitioning. It means to be seeking and to be asking and to be knocking on heaven's door. It means to be entreating. This is not Paul just going through a little checklist, a punch list of names of people who he needs to pray for, but Paul's heart is in it and he has identified with them in prayer for their salvation. And that is the way we must be as well.

And yet, here we see the very first verse in Romans chapter 10 is Paul says his heart's desire and his prayer to God for them is for their salvation, and he has just told us that their salvation has already been foreordained and predetermined from before the foundation of the world. And what I want us to see here is the fact that Romans chapter 9 in no way negates praying for the salvation of those who are lost. In fact, it actually motivates us to pray for the lost, because if God is not sovereign, you are just wasting your time in prayer. You need to go talk to lost people; don't talk to God if God is not involved in this and if God is not sovereign. The mere fact that God is sovereign in salvation means we should talk to God about this, because God is the only one who can intervene and overcome the resistance of the unbelief in the hearts of unbelievers. So, this is not inconsistent; this is perfectly consistent with the doctrine of sovereign election.[8]

The unselfishness of his praying is seen in his writing to the Romans where he tells them, "Making request if by any means I might have a prosperous journey to come to you. For I long to see you that I may impart to you some spiritual gift to the end ye may be established." The object of his desire to visit Rome was not for selfish gratification, the pleasure of a trip, or for other reasons, but that he might be the means under God of "imparting to them some spiritual gift," in order that they "might be established" in their hearts, unblamable in love. It was that his visit might give to them some spiritual gift which they had not received and that they might be established at those points where they needed to be rooted, and grounded in faith, in love, and in all that made up Christian life and character.

CONCLUSION

Paul not only prayed for himself. He made a practice of praying for others. He was preeminently an intercessor. Paul's prayer is that the Believer may know God intimately and affirms the truth and historical reality of their faith. In contrast to contemporary human

8. Steven J. Lawson. Prayer for the Lost—Romans 10:1–3 (http://www. onepassionministries.org/transcripts/2019/6/6/prayer-for-the-lost-romans-101-3) (accessed on 18th May, 2021).

centric intercession prayers of health and wealth, Paul's focus on the Jesus Christ, as the basis and instrument of God' plan of salvation, is to encourage the recognition of God's grace.

Again, I ask, what about you and me? How much effort are we putting forth to try and help others have an opportunity to hear the gospel? After we think about their salvation and pray about it, there is still one thing left to do: open our mouths and teach God's word like the early saints did (Acts 8:35). Paul's eyes were open to the spiritual needs of lost people. He once told King Agrippa, *"I would to God that not only you, but also all who hear me today, might become both almost and altogether such as I am, except for these chains"* (Acts 26:29). We can understand why he felt so strongly about his brethren in the flesh, but he zealously brought God's gospel to lost Gentiles as well. It is good for us to focus on particular individuals and make a concentrated effort to reach out to them with the gospel. At the same time, we must be mindful of teaching opportunities that come our way when we are not even searching for them. The lost are the lost, regardless of their gender, skin color, or nationality.

10

CONCLUSION: JESUS, THE GOD WHO INTERCEEDS FOR US

INTERCESSION MEANS TO "PLEAD on behalf of another." When the object of prayer is an appeal for God to help other people, this falls into the category of intercession. All believers are called to intercede for one another, such as the Apostle Paul told Timothy, *"I urge you, first of all, to pray for all people. Ask God to help them; intercede on their behalf, and give thanks for them"* (1 Timothy 2:1 NLT). Also, to the church at Ephesus, Paul wrote, *"Pray in the Spirit at all times and on every occasion. Stay alert and be persistent in your prayers for all believers everywhere."*[1]

In another instance, Paul wrote of his intercession for the believers at Colossae, *"For this reason we also, since the day we heard it, do not cease to pray for you, and to ask that you may be filled with the knowledge of His will in all wisdom and spiritual understanding"* (Colossians 1:9). He also requested their intercession for him, *"that God would open to us a door for the word, to speak the mystery of Christ"* (Colossians 4:3). And apparently, Epaphras, a colleague of Paul's in Rome, was also quite an intercessor, of whom Paul wrote, *"He is always wrestling in prayer for you, that*

---

1. Ephesians 6:18 (NLT).

you may stand firm in all the will of God, mature and fully assured" (Colossians 4:12 NIV).

Therefore, one can observe an incredible pattern in the whole Bible regarding God's intercessory ministry. It is very positive toward His people because He is for them, never against them, and wants to save. Intercessors are important because prayer is the means God uses to work in the behalf of others. While Jesus is the only mediator between God and man, standing at God's right hand interceding for us (1 Timothy 2:5, Romans 8:34), believers also serve as intermediaries to intercede and help reconcile souls to the life-changing truths of Jesus (2 Corinthians 5:18). In other words, the prayers of an intercessor helps "bridge the gap" in behalf of others. . . taking up the slack, adding strength to theirs, helping them make a connection. *"I sought for a man among them who would make a wall, and stand in the gap before Me on behalf of the land, that I should not destroy it; but I found no one"* (Ezekiel 22:30).

Intercession is something that all Christians are called to participate with. . . However, some believers feel a special calling, passion or anointing toward intercessory prayer and consider that their primary ministry. While prayer isn't specifically mentioned as a gift in scripture, "faith" certainly is (1 Corinthians 12:9), as well as other motivational-type gifts such as such as service, mercy or helps (Romans 12:3–7) . . . any of which may involve this kind of intercessory prayer.

The obvious key word of the nature of "intercession." Here are several definitions from some of the different Bible Dictionaries as to what the word "intercession" means:[2]

- Prayer offered in behalf of others
- To assail with urgent petitions, entreating God for His favor
- The act of petitioning God or praying on behalf of another person or group

---

2. Intercessory Ministries of Jesus Christ and the Holy Spirit (bible-knowledge.com) (accessed 27 March 2023).

- To reach, to meet someone, to pressure or urge someone strongly

- The act of intervening or mediating between differing parties, particularly the act of praying to God on behalf of another person

All of these definitions are showing us that whenever a person is interceding for another person before God the Father, they are literally praying for that other person and whatever their special prayer need may be at the time.

BIBLIOGRAPHY

Alister E. McGrath, *Christian Theology: An Introduction*. Cambridge, Mass.: Blackwell Publishers, 1997.

Anderson, G.W. *The Psalms,* in *Peak's Commentary on the Bible,* London, Routledge, First *Annotated Bible,* New York: Oxford University Press, 1977.

Anderson, G.W. *The Psalms, in Peak's Commentary on the Bible,* London, Routledge, First Publication in Paperback, 2001;

Brown C, ed., *The New International Dictionary of New Testament Theology,* vol. 2, Grand Rapids: Zondervan Publishing House, 1979.

Childs, Brevard. *Biblical Theology of the Old and New Testaments: Theological Reflection on the Christian Bible.* Minneapolis: Fortress Press, 1993.

Conner, Kevin J. *The Temple of Solomon.* City Bible Publishing, Portland, Oregon, 1988.

Searle, David. "Who is David's Mother" in *Rutherford Journal of Church and Ministry,* (Claremont, Edinburg: Rutherford House 1994), 16–17.

Dentan, Robert, C. "Psalms" in Bruce M. Metzger and R.E. Murphy, eds., *The New Oxford Annotated Bible,* New York: Oxford University Press, 1977;

Desmond Alexander, *The Rutherford Journal of Church and Ministry,* 17.

Doughteen, Russell, S. "Chapter 1: Presenting Bible Prophecy Through Fiction." in *Revelation Hoofbeats,* edited by Ron J. Bigalke, Jr. Eternal Ministries, 2003.

Dunn, James D. G., ed. (2003), *The Cambridge Companion to St. Paul,* Cambridge: Cambridge University Press,2003.

Estes, Daniel J. *Handbook on the Wisdom Books and Psalms: Job, Psalms, Proverbs, Ecclesiastes, Song of Songs.* Baker Academic: A Division of Baker Publishing Group, Grand Rapids, MI., 2005.

Frank G. Carver, "The Quest for the Holy: The Darkness of God" in *Wesleyan Theological Journal, Volume 23, Number 1 and 2* (Spring-Fall, 1988).

Gaebelein F, ed., *The Expositor's Bible Commentary: Ephesians through Philippians,* Grand Rapids: Zondervan Publishing House, 1992.

Guzik, David. *Psalm 90—The Prayer of Moses in the Wilderness.* Enduring Word Bible Commentary, Psalm 90, 2016.

BIBLIOGRAPHY

Blenkinsopp, Joseph. *Wisdom and Law in the Old Testament: The Ordering of Life in Israel and Early Judaism* (Oxford: Oxford University Press, 1995).

Kitchen, K. A. *Ancient Orient and Old Testament.* Chicago: Inter-Varity, 1966.

Kselman, J.S. and Barre, M.L. "Psalms" in *NJBC,* New York: Geoffrey Chapman, 1995;

Maddox, Randy. *Responsible Grace: John Wesley's Practical Theology* (Nashville, Tennessee: Kingswood Books, 1994).

McBride, S.D. "Polity of the Covenant People: The Book of Deuteronomy," *Interpretation* 41 (1987), 229–44.

McCullough, W.S. "Psalms: An Introduction" *The Interpreter's Bible in Twelve Volumes,* IV, Twenty-5th Printing, Nashville: Abingdon, 1978;

Michael Lodahl, *The Story of God: Wesleyan Theological and Biblical Narrative,* (Kansas City, MO. Beacon Hill Press, 1994), 76–79.

Michael, White. *From Jesus to Christianity.* San Francisco, CA: HarperCollins, 2007.

Mowinckel, Sigmund, *The Psalms in Israel's Worship in Two Volumes,* trans, by D.R.A. P Publication in Paperback, 2001.

Mvula, Hermann Y. *The Theory, Praxis and Pursuit of Constitutionalism in Democratic Malawi.* Kachere Series, Zomba, 2020.

Mvula, Hermann Y. "Toward a Theology that Responds to Governance and Political Processes in Malawi: A Biblical Perspective from the Book of Deuteronomy," in *Decolonizing the Theological Curriculum in an Online Age,* edited by Felix Nyika, Hermann Mvula and Ken Ross. Zomba: Theological Society of Malawi, 2022.

Randy Maddox, *Responsible Grace: John Wesley's Practical theology* (Nashville, TN: Kingswood Books, 1994.

Raymond, Dillard B. Word Biblical Commentary, Volume 15: 2 Chronicles. Dallas, Texas: Word Books, Publisher. 1998.

Richard Boyce, *"The Cry to God in the Old Testament." SBL Dissertation Series,* 103. Atlanta: Scholars Press, 1988.

Searle, David. "Who was David's Mother?" *Rutherford Journal of Church and Ministry.* Thomas Nashville: Abingdon, 1962.

Walter Martin, *Kingdom of the Cults,* edited by Ravi Zacharias. Minneapolis, Bethany House Publishers, 2003.

Walvoord JF and Zuck RB, eds., *Bible Knowledge Commentary,* Wheaton: Victor Books, 1985.

Wright, Christopher. J.H. *Living as the People of God: The Relevance of Old Testament Ethics.* Leicester: Inter-Varsity Press, 1983.

Wright, Christopher J.H. *Deuteronomy.* Grand Rapids, MI: Baker Books, 1996.

Wright, Ernest. *Great People of the Bible and How they Lived.* Canada: The Readers Digest Association, 1974.

INTERNET SOURCES

Dennis, Olson, "Exodus 32:1–14 Commentary" (Accessed from http://www.biblia.work/sermons/exodus-321-14-commentary-by-dennis-olson/ (accessed on 26th February, 2018).

Guzik, David. "Psalm 90—The Prayer of Moses in the Wilderness" (*Enduring Word Bible Commentary*, Psalm 90, 2016) (accessed on 5th March, 2021).

John W. Ritenbaugh, "What the Bible says about Education of Moses" (bibletools.org) (accessed on 22 March 2023).

Steven J. Lawson, Steven. Prayer for the Lost - Romans 10:1–3 (http://www.onepassionministries.org/transcripts/2019/6/6/prayer-for-the-lost-romans-101-3) (accessed on 18th May, 2021).

https://www.google.com/search?q=Did+the+apostle+Peter+go+to+babylon&oq=Did+the+apostle+Peter+go+to+babylon&aqs=chrome..69i57.13158joj7&sourcei) (accessed on 24th https://www.billkochman.com/Articles/AMysterySolvedPeterBabylon.html (December 26, 2016).

https://bible.org/article/book-ezra (accessed on 18th May, 2021)

https://bible.org/seriespage/lesson-9-godly-reaction-sin-ezra-91–15 (accessed on 18th

http://www.thewordisalive.co.uk/OT/Exodus/Exodus32.pdf (Accessed on 26th February, 2018).

http://www.thewordisalive.co.uk/OT/Exodus/Exodus32.pdf (Accessed on 26th

http://www.thewordisalive.co.uk/OT/Exodus/Exodus32.pdf (accessed on 26th February 2018).

Judaism: Founder, Beliefs (https://www.history.com) (accessed on 5th March, 2021).

BBC-Religions-Judaism (https://www.bbc.co.uk) (accessed on 5th March, 2021).

"Did Moses Write Psalm 90? –Biblical Hermeneutics Stack Exchange" (s.stackexchange.com) (accessed on 5th March, 2021).